Teamwork Test Prep

READING

GRADE

7

by Drew Johnson and
Cynthia Johnson

Illustrations by Marty Bucella

Carson-Dellosa Publishing Company, Inc.
Greensboro, North Carolina

Credits

Authors: Drew Johnson and Cynthia Johnson
Editors: Kelly Morris Huxmann, Sabena Maiden, and Karen Seberg
Layout Design: Mark Conrad
Production: River Road Graphics
Inside Illustrations: Marty Bucella
Cover Design: Annette Hollister-Papp

Table of Contents

 # Introduction

Across the country, thousands of students and teachers spend countless hours preparing for state standardized tests. This focus on repetitive, high-intensity preparation can increase student anxiety, cause "burnout," and lead students to develop strong negative feelings about testing—all undesirable effects that can ultimately hurt students' test performance.

Teamwork Test Prep offers a change of pace. This book provides fun, creative group activities that sharpen students' test-taking abilities, build their confidence, instill positive attitudes toward the tests they are facing, and provide them with a supportive network of classmates who share their goals.

Teamwork Test Prep is an effective alternative to the drills and drudgery often associated with the process of getting students ready for standardized tests. It provides everything you need to transform test preparation from a necessary chore into a group experience that is rewarding in its own right. Here is what you will find inside this book:

✗ A short history of the rise of state testing programs

✗ A list of resources where you can find more information about your state's tests and learning standards

✗ An explanation of our unique "teamwork" approach to test preparation and your key role as "coach"

✗ A short, diagnostic reading test to measure your students' current abilities and gauge their progress

✗ Important test-taking skills and strategies that students can really use

✗ Engaging group activities specifically designed to hone important comprehension skills

✗ A practice test to help students prepare for the real thing

Use *Teamwork Test Prep* as a self-contained test preparation program, or supplement your existing program with the activities and diagnostics in this book. Either approach is sure to give your students a boost—in their scores, spirits, and confidence!

Understanding Your State's Tests

Understanding the issues involved with state assessment tests is the first step in preparing your students for success. Although standards may vary from state to state, many important issues are common to all states when it comes to standardized testing. The practical information found in this chapter can be used by teachers anywhere in the United States. It includes:

X The basic components of the No Child Left Behind Act

X An overview of the test development process at the state level

X A checklist of questions to help you familiarize yourself with your state's tests

X Valuable resources you can use to gather more information about your state's tests

The No Child Left Behind Act

Passed in January 2002, the No Child Left Behind Act (NCLB) represents the federal government's most recent plan for education reform. The centerpiece of the law mandates annual testing in math and reading, beginning in 2005, for all public school students in grades three through eight. Although this is a federal mandate, the government has not established a concurrent set of national standards that all states must follow. Instead, states have the flexibility to create their own "statewide accountability systems." Within these systems, each state typically:

X Sets academic standards in each content area for what students should learn and master at each grade level

X Develops tests that are aligned with the state standards

X Uses those tests to collect objective data to analyze how students are doing (Often this data is delineated to show how various socioeconomic subsets are faring in the educational system.)

X Makes improvements in curriculum, instruction, and assessment on the basis of test results

Whatever systems a state chooses to develop and follow, it is ultimately held responsible for the performance of its students. Students must perform at a proficient level—according to each state's standards—within 12 years of NCLB's enactment. Each state must also share its data or test results with local communities in the form of reports. These reports are designed to inform parents and other stakeholders of how student learning is measuring up to the state's standards and educational goals. Consequences of the testing results may differ from state to state. In one state, a low-performing district that shows no improvement might have its superintendent replaced, while in another, a school with continued "failing" grades might find itself taken over by the state education agency.

Since many states already have some form of state testing in place, the passage of No Child Left Behind has not drastically changed current testing patterns. Tests are being revamped, however, to meet NCLB requirements. Since each state has flexibility in setting its own standards, the tests students will take are likely to reflect what they may already know or are currently learning. For example, a standardized reading test established for seventh graders in Utah would be relevant for students in that state, but not necessarily for seventh graders in New Hampshire.

How State Assessment Tests Are Developed

The first step in developing state assessment tests is to establish learning standards. This helps ensure equal learning opportunities for all students and, thus, equal opportunities for academic achievement. Standards are usually divided by grade level and content area, or discipline; and some are further divided by course number or subdiscipline. These standards form the basis of the scope and sequence of skills assessed, and, in some cases, delineate actual content covered, as in social studies or science.

Standards developed in each state set the tone for instruction and achievement. Most state standards reflect carefully derived expectations of what students should know and be able to do at a specific grade level. These expectations of proficiency also establish curriculum frameworks. Educators use these standards as a scaffolding to determine the skills, content, and processes that students should learn.

After the standards are established, the actual test development process begins. Although the process varies from state to state, test development generally goes through several stages. Each state's department of education or state educational agency has a specific internal department or division dedicated to curriculum development and assessment. This group of professional educators first evaluates any previous state assessments to see how well they measure current or newly adopted standards. Then, through analysis of similar or previously administered exams and current assessment research, these educators develop testing blueprints to best represent the core standards and essential elements of the curriculum.

The next stage for most states involves developing a field test based on the blueprints. Field tests are written and administered to try out items that may be used later on actual tests. After the field tests have been administered, review committees evaluate the results to determine the appropriateness, accuracy, and alignment of test items.

Benchmark tests may also be developed to set the scoring goals for new assessments or standards. Like field tests, benchmark tests are scored and recorded, but they are not used for accountability purposes at the district, school, or student level. These tests are used to see how well students will perform on the final tests and to help guide instruction.

The actual writing of the tests can vary depending on the state. Some states develop the tests completely within their own education departments. Assessment specialists review and revise test items, which are written by professional item writers hired independently by the education department. Some states, such as Texas and New York, hire former or current teachers to develop test items based on blueprints created by their education departments.

In other states, the tests are outsourced and written by professional educational testing companies that have contracted with the state. Test items are written by company-hired professional writers or, in some cases, by professional writers collaborating with education department staff. These writers use the previously developed test blueprints as guidelines for writing. Each item is written to measure specific content standards and then reviewed by the state's education department for alignment and accuracy.

Once benchmark tests have been developed and administered to students, a passing standard is established based on the results. This passing standard is used to compare how well students should perform versus how well they actually do perform on the real tests.

Finally, the real tests are developed and administered to students. If students do not perform at or above the passing standard, schools use the results to examine factors that may help improve students' scores and, along with them, academic achievement.

Checklist: What You Need to Know about Your State's Tests

Having the information you need about your own state's tests is crucial to your students' achievement. Luckily, this information is readily available. Use the following checklist of questions as a guide in learning about your state's standards and assessment tests:

- ☐ What are the learning standards for each major content area per grade level?
- ☐ What is the most current form of state assessment test administered at each grade level?
- ☐ What is the state's time frame for developing and administering new assessment tests?
- ☐ What is the schedule of testing dates for each grade level?
- ☐ How are the standards assessed per test, per grade level?
- ☐ What scoring and rating systems are used for the tests?
- ☐ How and when are testing "report cards" disseminated?
- ☐ Is there any additional pre- and post-testing data available?
- ☐ What test preparation materials are available? (test samples, instructional materials, benchmark or other practice tests, etc.)
- ☐ What training is available at the school, district, state, and regional levels for teachers and parents?
- ☐ What are the implications and consequences of the test results for students, teachers, schools, and districts?
- ☐ Who composes the tests and what input may you have on their design?
- ☐ What local, state, regional, and national resources are available that address standardized testing? (organizations, educational boards and agencies, advocacy and research groups, professional and community listservs, Web-based bulletin boards, etc.)
- ☐ Whom can you contact at the school or district level for more information? (school dean of instruction, instructional specialist, department chairperson, other administrators, etc.)

The Information You Need: Resources for State Standards and Assessment

Much of the information for the checklist on page 7 is available from the following resources:

National Resources

No Child Left Behind Act Web site
http://www.ed.gov/nclb/landing.jhtml
> This Web site includes separate sections for students, parents, teachers, and administrators. It addresses testing, accountability, reading issues, teachers' roles, and much more. The site also provides links to an E-mail based subscription newsletter, details on policy and legislation, fact sheets, statistics and graphs, state testing information, and additional resources.

United States Department of Education
http://www.ed.gov/index.jhtml
> This site contains information for students, parents, teachers, and administrators on educational priorities, research and statistics, PreK–12 issues, as well as links to other educational resources.

National Education Association
http://www.nea.org/
> The NEA's site includes information on accountability and testing, help for parents, a legislative action center link, various publications, and current educational news.

Education News
http://www.educationnews.org/
> This Web site offers free, education-related information from all states, complete with daily headline stories and a searchable archive.

Teachvision.com
http://www.teachervision.fen.com/lesson-plans/lesson-10279.html
> This site provides an extensive list of resources on No Child Left Behind.

State Education Departments/Agencies

An asterisk (*) denotes a special Web site outlining standards/assessments if available.

Alabama Department of Education
50 North Ripley Street
P.O. Box 302101
Montgomery, AL 36104
Phone: (334) 242-9700
http://www.alsde.edu/html/home.asp

Alaska Department of Education and
   Early Development
801 West Tenth Street, Suite 200
Juneau, AK 99801-1878
Phone: (907) 465-2800
Fax: (907) 465-3452
http://www.educ.state.ak.us/home.html
* *http://www.educ.state.ak.us/standards/*
* *http://www.educ.state.ak.us/tls/assessment/*

Arizona Department of Education
1535 West Jefferson Street
Phoenix, AZ 85007
Phone: (602) 542-5393 or (800) 352-4558
http://www.ade.state.az.us/
* *http://www.ade.state.az.us/standards/*

Arkansas Department of Education
#4 Capitol Mall
Little Rock, AR 72201
Phone: (501) 682-4475
http://arkedu.state.ar.us/
* *http://arkedu.state.ar.us/actaap/index.htm*

California Department of Education
1430 N Street
Sacramento, CA 95814
Phone: (916) 319-0800
http://goldmine.cde.ca.gov/
* *http://goldmine.cde.ca.gov/statetests/*

Colorado Department of Education
201 East Colfax Avenue
Denver, CO 80203-1799
Phone: (303) 866-6600
Fax: (303) 830-0793
http://www.cde.state.co.us/index_home.htm
* *http://www.cde.state.co.us/index_stnd.htm*

Connecticut State Department of Education
165 Capitol Avenue
Hartford, CT 06145
Phone: (860) 713-6548
http://www.state.ct.us/sde/

Delaware Department of Education
401 Federal Street
P.O. Box 1402
Dover, DE 19903-1402
Phone: (302) 739-4601
Fax: (302) 739-4654
http://www.doe.state.de.us/index.htm
* *http://www.doe.state.de.us/AAB/*

Florida Department of Education
Office of the Commissioner
Turlington Building, Suite 1514
325 West Gaines Street
Tallahassee, FL 32399
Phone: (850) 245-0505
Fax: (850) 245-9667
http://www.fldoe.org/
* *http://www.firn.edu/doe/curric/prek12/*
  frame2.htm

Georgia Department of Education
2054 Twin Towers East
Atlanta, GA 30334
Phone: (404) 656-2800 or (800) 311-3627
Fax: (404) 651-6867
http://www.doe.k12.ga.us/index.asp
* Georgia Learning Connections Web site:
  http://www.glc.k12.ga.us/
  GLC Phone: (404) 651-5664
  GLC Fax: (404) 657-5183

Hawaii Department of Education
1390 Miller Street
P.O. Box 2360
Honolulu, HI 96804
Phone: (808) 586-3230
Fax: (808) 586-3234
http://doe.k12.hi.us/
* *http://doe.k12.hi.us/standards/index.htm*

Idaho Department of Education
650 West State Street
P.O. Box 83720
Boise, ID 83720-0027
Phone: (208) 332-6800
http://www.sde.state.id.us/Dept/
* *http://www.sde.state.id.us/admin/standards/*

Illinois State Board of Education
100 North First Street
Springfield, IL 62777-0001
Phone: (217) 782-4321 or (866) 262-6663
Fax: (217) 524-4928
TTY: (217) 782-1900
http://www.isbe.state.il.us/
* *http://www.isbe.state.il.us/ils/*

Indiana Department of Education
Room 229, State House
Indianapolis, IN 46204-2798
Phone: (317) 232-6610
Fax: (317) 232-8004
http://doe.state.in.us/welcome.html
* *http://doe.state.in.us/asap/welcome.html*

Iowa Department of Education
Grimes State Office Building
Des Moines, IA 50319-0146
Phone: (515) 281-5294
Fax: (515) 242-5988
http://www.state.ia.us/educate/index.html
* *http://www.state.ia.us/educate/ecese/nclb/doc/*
  ccsb.html

Kansas State Department of Education
120 SE Tenth Avenue
Topeka, KS 66612-1182
Phone: (785) 296-3201
Fax: (785) 296-7933
http://www.ksbe.state.ks.us/Welcome.html
* *http://www.ksbe.state.ks.us/assessment/
   index.html*

Kentucky Department of Education
500 Mero Street
Frankfort, KY 40601
Phone: (502) 564-4770 or (800) 533-5372
TTY: (502) 564-4970
http://www.kde.state.ky.us/

Louisiana Department of Education
P.O. Box 94064
Baton Rouge, LA 70804-9064
Phone: (877) 453-2721
http://www.doe.state.la.us/
* *http://www.doe.state.la.us/doecd/reaching.asp*

Maine Department of Education
23 State House Station
Augusta, ME 04333-0023
Phone: (207) 624-6774
Fax: (207) 624-6771
http://www.state.me.us/education/
* *http://www.state.me.us/education/lres/
   homepage.htm*

Maryland State Department of Education
200 West Baltimore Street
Baltimore, MD 21201
Phone: (410) 767-0100
http://marylandpublicschools.org/
* *http://mdk12.org/*

Massachusetts Department of Education
350 Main Street
Malden, MA 02148-5023
Phone: (781) 338-3000
http://www.doe.mass.edu/
* *http://www.doe.mass.edu/frameworks/current.html*

Michigan Department of Education
608 West Allegan
Lansing, MI 48933
Phone: (517) 373-3324
http://michigan.gov/mde/

Minnesota Department of Education
1500 Highway 36 West
Roseville, MN 55113-4266
Phone: (651) 582-8200
*http://www.education.state.mn.us/html/mde_
home.htm*

Mississippi Department of Education
Central High School
P.O. Box 771
359 North West Street
Jackson, MS 39205
Phone: (601) 359-3513
http://www.mde.k12.ms.us/
* *http://marcopolo.mde.k12.ms.us/
   frameworks.html*

Missouri Department of Elementary and
   Secondary Education
P.O. Box 480
Jefferson City, MO 65102
Phone: (573) 751-4212
Fax: (573) 751-8613
http://www.dese.state.mo.us/
* *http://www.dese.state.mo.us/standards/*

Montana Office of Public Instruction
P.O. Box 202501
Helena, MT 59620-2501
Phone: (406) 444-3095 or (888) 231-9393
http://www.opi.state.mt.us/
* *http://www.opi.state.mt.us/Standards/Index.html*

Nebraska Department of Education
301 Centennial Mall South
Lincoln, NE 68509
Phone: (402) 471-2295
http://www.nde.state.ne.us/
* *http://www.nde.state.ne.us/AcadStand.html*

Nevada Department of Education
700 East Fifth Street
Carson City, NV 89701
Phone: (775) 687-9200
Fax: (775) 687-9101
http://www.nde.state.nv.us/
* *http://www.nde.state.nv.us/sca/standards/*
   index.html

New Hampshire Department of Education
101 Pleasant Street
Concord, NH 03301-3860
Phone: (603) 271-3494
Fax: (603) 271-1953
http://www.ed.state.nh.us/
* *http://www.ed.state.nh.us/Curriculum*
   Frameworks/curricul.htm

New Jersey Department of Education
P.O. Box 500
Trenton, NJ 08625
Phone: (609) 292-4469
http://www.state.nj.us/education/index.html
* *http://www.state.nj.us/njded/stass/index.html*

New Mexico Public Education Department
300 Don Gaspar
Santa Fe, NM 87501-2786
Phone: (505) 827-5800
http://www.sde.state.nm.us/
* *http://164.64.166.11/cilt/standards/*

New York State Education Department
89 Washington Avenue
Albany, NY 12234
Phone: (518) 474-3852
http://www.nysed.gov/home.html
* *http://www.nysatl.nysed.gov/standards.html*

North Carolina Department of
   Public Instruction
301 North Wilmington Street
Raleigh, NC 27601
Phone: (919) 807-3300
http://www.ncpublicschools.org/
* *http://www.ncpublicschools.org/curriculum/*

North Dakota Department of
   Public Instruction
600 East Boulevard Avenue
Department 201
Floors 9, 10, and 11
Bismarck, ND 58505-0440
Phone: (701) 328-2260
Fax: (701) 328-2461
http://www.dpi.state.nd.us/index.shtm
* *http://www.dpi.state.nd.us/standard/index.shtm*

Ohio Department of Education
25 South Front Street
Columbus, OH 43215-4183
Phone: (877) 644-6338
http://www.ode.state.oh.us/
* *http://www.ode.state.oh.us/academic_*
   content_standards/

Oklahoma State Department of Education
2500 North Lincoln Boulevard
Oklahoma City, OK 73105-4599
Phone: (405) 521-3301
Fax: (405) 521-6205
http://www.sde.state.ok.us/home/defaultie.html

Oregon Department of Education
255 Capitol Street NE
Salem, OR 97310-0203
Phone: (503) 378-3569
TDD: (503) 378-2892
Fax: (503) 378-5156
http://www.ode.state.or.us/
* *http://www.ode.state.or.us/asmt/standards/*

Pennsylvania Department of Education
333 Market Street
Harrisburg, PA 17126
Phone: (717) 783-6788
http://www.pde.state.pa.us/pde_internet/site/
default.asp
* *http://www.pde.state.pa.us/stateboard_ed/*
   *cwp/view.asp?a = 3&Q = 76716&stateboard_*
   edNav = |5467|

Rhode Island Department of Education
255 Westminster Street
Providence, RI 02903
Phone: (401) 222-4600
http://www.ridoe.net/
* *http://www.ridoe.net/standards/frameworks/
default.htm*

South Carolina Department of Education
1429 Senate Street
Columbia, SC 29201
Phone: (803) 734-8815
Fax: (803) 734-3389
http://www.myscschools.com/
* *http://www.myscschools.com/offices/cso/*

South Dakota Department of Education
700 Governors Drive
Pierre, SD 57501
http://www.state.sd.us/deca/Index.htm
* *http://www.state.sd.us/deca/OCTA/
contentstandards/index.htm*

Tennessee Department of Education
Andrew Johnson Tower, 6th Floor
Nashville, TN 37243-0375
Phone: (615) 741-2731
http://www.state.tn.us/education/
* *http://www.state.tn.us/education/ci/
cistandards.htm*

Texas Education Agency
1701 North Congress Avenue
Austin, TX 78701
Phone: (512) 463-9734
http://www.tea.state.tx.us/
* *http://www.tea.state.tx.us/teks/index.html*
* *http://www.tea.state.tx.us/student.assessment/
teachers.html*

Utah State Office of Education
250 East 500 South
P.O. Box 144200
Salt Lake City, UT 84114-4200
Phone: (801) 538-7500
http://www.usoe.k12.ut.us/
* *http://www.uen.org/core/*

Vermont Department of Education
120 State Street
Montpelier, VT 05620-2501
http://www.state.vt.us/educ/
* *http://www.state.vt.us/educ/new/html/pubs/
framework.html*

Virginia Department of Education
P.O. Box 2120
Richmond, VA 23218
Phone: (800) 292-3820
http://www.pen.k12.va.us/
* *http://www.pen.k12.va.us/VDOE/Instruction/
sol.html*

Washington Office of the Superintendent of
Public Instruction (OSPI)
Old Capitol Building
P.O. Box 47200
Olympia, WA 98504-7200
Phone: (360) 725-6000
TTY: (360) 664-3631
http://www.k12.wa.us/
* *http://www.k12.wa.us/curriculuminstruct/*

West Virginia Department of Education
1900 Kanawha Boulevard East
Charleston, WV 25305
Phone: (304) 558-3660
Fax: (304) 558-0198
http://wvde.state.wv.us/

Wisconsin Department of Public Instruction
125 South Webster Street
P.O. Box 7841
Madison, WI 53707-7841
Phone: (608) 266-3390 or (800) 441-4563
http://www.dpi.state.wi.us/index.html
* *http://www.dpi.state.wi.us/dpi/dlsis/
currinst.html*

Wyoming Department of Education
2300 Capitol Avenue
Hathaway Building, 2nd Floor
Cheyenne, WY 82002-0050
Phone: (307) 777-7675
Fax: (307) 777-6234
http://www.k12.wy.us/index.asp
* *http://www.k12.wy.us/eqa/nca/pubs/
standards.asp*

Introducing the Tests to Your Students

Before tackling any new task, it is a good idea to come up with a game plan for how to proceed. Figuring out a game plan and conveying it to your students can make the task of test taking seem more manageable and even fun!

This book outlines the steps for a game plan and gives you the tools you will need along the way, including innovative activities and sample test questions. However, the approach you use in preparing your students will be key to their success. This book's game plan is designed to draw upon your strengths as an encouraging and motivating teacher—in short, as a testing "coach."

Chapter 2 explains how to get students started on the right foot. It shows you how to present state standardized tests as important challenges students can train for as a team.

The Coach Approach

The activities in this book are designed to build upon and enhance skills that are assessed on state standardized tests in a way that is active, engaging, and fun. Remember—test preparation does not have to be boring. Move beyond the usual "skill and drill" and get creative in your approach to teaching. Adopting the persona of coach can make all the difference in tackling the challenges your students face with these important tests. Using the coach approach can help eliminate test anxiety, build confidence, develop skills, and increase motivation.

Attitude Check

Coaching can be viewed as the application of teaching strategies to a set of activities that introduce, reinforce, and synthesize skills that players (students) need to perform their best. The role involves juggling many tasks at once. As a coach, you are an instructor, a facilitator, a motivator, a troubleshooter, and a supporter, all in one. The role also implies a strong desire to do the job and do it well.

Before developing your coach persona, it is crucial to evaluate how you feel about and approach standardized tests. A teacher's attitude and nonverbal messages can have a big impact on students, whether intentional or not. You may have quite a few legitimate gripes about the amount of time required for testing and preparation, the design of the tests, and the sometimes questionable uses of test scores. Regardless of these issues, take a moment to reflect on the following questions related to testing:

1. As a student, how did you feel about testing? Were you confident, careless, or anxious?
2. How do you feel about taking time from (or building time within) the curriculum to address test preparation?
3. How do you feel when testing results are published and available?
4. What can you do to make the testing process productive for you and your students?

Use your responses to these questions as the first steps in establishing your coaching character.

Putting On Your Game Face

As a good coach, you will motivate your students to perform their best, giving them the confidence to work on skills that need improvement. Coaching is a long-term process, requiring both dedication and flexibility. A successful coach will be:

- ✗ Patient
- ✗ Positive
- ✗ Motivated
- ✗ Resourceful
- ✗ Creative

Just as the students will work on skills where needed, so will you. As you regularly think about and use essential coaching skills, you will continue to gain confidence with them.

Suiting up as a coach does not mean shedding all of your qualities as a teacher. One way to help unite these two important roles is to evaluate how test preparation draws upon core teaching skills and instructional objectives. Since all state standardized tests are based on curriculum standards, look at the tests through the lens of authentic assessment. The tests are the outcomes of skills and content students are already learning rather than extraneous hurdles for students to overcome. Try to view test preparation as an opportunity to incorporate innovative strategies, diverse activities, and alternative approaches to content into your curriculum. This will allow you to prepare students for the tests without losing sight of the fundamentals of learning and quality instruction.

Use this perspective to develop a positive outlook toward the tests, and your attitude will be obvious to your students. To foster the same attitude among students, try to convey the importance of the tests to them—not just in terms of assessment, but also in terms of their development as learners. Describe both the purpose and outcomes of the tests in terms of what students will gain from them. Explain to students that the tests will help them focus their learning, shape up some of their academic skills, and give them opportunities to demonstrate what they have learned. Students will train for the tests like professional athletes training for a competition. Then, on the big day, they will have a chance to demonstrate just how good they really are.

Synonymous with coaching is motivating. To get yourself in a motivational frame of mind, try to view the upcoming tests as academic challenges rather than obstacles. Transfer this energy to students by encouraging them to think of each test as a big game for which they are preparing. Try to develop a team spirit in the class. Talk to students about how you are going to give them the techniques, strategies, and experience they need to achieve peak performance. When introducing any of the activities provided in this book, explain exactly how each activity will make students better, stronger test-takers.

A resourceful coach is one who does not see limits, but rather possibilities or alternatives. If one strategy does not work, try something else or modify the strategy to meet the needs of your players. If some of the activities or strategies outlined in this book do not seem to "click" with students, use your creative sensibilities to revise them to better suit your students' needs.

Devising a Game Plan

A good coach plans ahead in order to prepare the team for victory. After you have determined your individual approach to coaching, the next step is to develop a game plan. A successful game plan will include activities and exercises targeted to the particular needs of the team. By focusing on areas where students need a boost, you will help them evolve from a scrappy set of inexperienced players to an accomplished team of testing aces. Here is an overview of the instructional game plan outlined in this book:

✗ Assess students' abilities through a diagnostic test (Chapter 3).

✗ Set realistic goals for the team based on diagnostic results.

✗ Use goals to develop objectives for skill development.

✗ Break down skills into accessible segments by using specific reading activities (Chapter 5).

✗ Involve the team in new approaches that use more than one skill at a time (Chapter 5).

✗ Simulate the game environment through test scrimmages and practice testing scenarios (Chapters 3 and 6).

✗ Incorporate strategies that help boost skills and performance (Chapter 4).

✗ Evaluate the process and teach students how to evaluate what they are doing (Chapter 4).

Before devising a training program, the coach must discern where the players are and where they need to go in order to be successful. That is why we recommend starting your program with the checklist and diagnostic test in Chapter 3. By first assessing your students' skills and their familiarity with the format of standardized tests, you will be able to formulate an appropriate and realistic plan to help them best prepare for the tests ahead. Using this plan, you can then select suitable activities to work on particular skills and present meaningful strategies for students to apply during the tests.

When introducing your state's reading test to students, establish your role as coach from the beginning. Explain that you will be working with the students to figure out where they are in order to get them where they should be before the "big game." Make it clear that along the way, you will be showing them several strategies they can use in their weaker areas when they feel trapped with the ball, so to speak.

Describe the test not as something impossible to beat, but as something that students can handle on their own. The training program you are developing, based on the students' "pre-event trial" (the diagnostic test in Chapter 3) will help prepare them well for the test. Explain that you will also help them stay motivated and maintain a positive attitude toward the test throughout the program. Make it clear that you welcome any ideas they may have to make the process more fun and less tedious.

Cross Training in the Classroom

Since you want to avoid burnout that can happen through basic drill instruction, and since you are an innovative coach by nature, try cross training your academic athletes.

In the usual sense, cross training means varying a regular exercise routine with different forms of exercise to reach the same goal. For example, soccer players may lift weights, football players may take up ballet, and runners may try bicycling to vary their workouts. These different types of activities give athletes new strengths and skills that make them better at their primary sports.

Cross training is an important facet of the coaching philosophy. It can easily be applied to training your students to face testing challenges. Drilling students with practice questions is an important part of test preparation, but it can become monotonous and boring. Cross training can keep students from getting bored. If students are given a variety of methods for developing testing skills, they will learn to apply their skills in different contexts, adapt their strategies to different activities, and synthesize these skills and strategies more naturally when performing on tests. Chapters 4 and 5 of this book address methods of cross training and provide ways to change up the normal "training program" for your students. Here are a few suggestions taken from those chapters:

X Intermingle straight drills with activities.

X Use different or unusual content to teach skills that cross disciplines.
(For example, use a popular song, magazine ad, or science article to teach students how to find the main idea.)

X Engage students in activities that practice and develop more than one skill at a time.

X Weave into the training program methods students can use to deal with test anxiety.

X Avoid overtraining by taking breaks. Plan "rest days" where the goal is to have fun learning something new or trying something different, rather than simply mastering another skill.

A beginning team may need to start with simple objectives before moving up to the goal of winning or beating the opponent. From this standpoint, building upon individual skills incrementally may be an approach you will want to try with your students. Having students exercise many skills at once can also keep tedium on the sidelines while encouraging a more integrated application that reflects the real world. This book provides some activities that focus on just one particular standard or skill, as well as others that tie related skills together in integrated ways.

The Mental Game: Motivation, Metacognition, and Modeling

One of the most important aspects of coaching is motivation. Motivated students have an edge when faced with any academic challenge. Give your students plenty of compelling reasons to want to do well on state tests and boost their self-confidence by preparing them thoroughly. If they want to do well for themselves and believe they can learn new skills, students will be well prepared and focused on testing days.

Coaching also involves constant evaluation—of progress, of problems, and of the process itself. Helping students develop metacognitive skills, or making them aware of their own processes and progress, will pay off enormously. Use the test-taking strategies in Chapter 4 to teach your students how to think about what they are doing while they are doing it and to identify their own strengths and weaknesses. Encourage them to use their minds to reduce anxiety and alleviate fears about testing. Using metacognition throughout the test-preparation process will help students stay focused and remain in control during the tests.

Another way to help students psych themselves up for testing is to model a positive attitude toward the process. Try not to let any frustrations you may have about the tests dampen your students' motivation. Encourage team spirit by talking about each test as a big game. Explain that you are going to prepare the students by giving them the techniques, strategies, and experiences needed to give a peak performance. And when introducing the activities in this book, describe exactly how they will help students become better, stronger test takers.

Standardized tests are a fact a life for students today. Your job as a coach is to teach them how to tackle those tests with confidence. You can remove the often crippling obstacles of anxiety and uncertainty from your students' paths, but it will take some work. The activities, strategies, and sample tests in this book, coupled with your own persistence and creativity as a coach, will all work together to boost students' skills and confidence.

How Coaching Looks in the Classroom

Since coaching is an active and involved role, any instruction related to your state's standardized tests should be, too. The activities in this book reflect this hands-on approach and provide lots of modeling potential. Each activity has been broken down into the following categories, allowing you to guide students through it step-by-step: Skills/State Standards, Description, Materials You Need, Getting Ready, Introducing the Activity, Modeling the Activity, Activity in Practice, and Extensions.

The activities are designed for collaborative pair or group work. However, many are adaptable and can be used with individual students for more focused skill instruction. No matter how you decide to use them, the activities are student-centered in nature, allowing you, the coach, to facilitate and assess while students actively develop their skills.

Identifying Problem Areas

In order to develop a program that will bring your students to peak performance on state assessment tests, begin by identifying any problem areas in their skill development. This will save you time and energy in the long run, and make the whole experience of preparing for the tests more advantageous for students. The short reading test included in this chapter is representative of seventh-grade state assessment tests. It can be used as a diagnostic tool to help pinpoint areas in which students need work.

Before administering the diagnostic test, it may be helpful to determine what exposure your students already have to the look, feel, and content of your state's tests. Think about what they do in the classroom that addresses test preparation in some way. Since your state's standards serve as the scaffolding for the curriculum, students should already be learning the content and developing the skills that will be assessed on the tests. However, they may not necessarily realize that what they are learning directly connects to the tests they will take. Use the following checklist of questions to review the key elements of the tests in connection with your students' current testing knowledge.

Checklist: Evaluating Your Students' Testing Savvy

General Questions

☐ Do students have experience with multiple-choice tests?

☐ How often do students read or write silently in class?

☐ How often do students take tests individually?

☐ What forms of standardized tests have students taken this year or previously?

☐ Do students have frequent practice using answer sheets to record their answers?

Reading Questions

☐ How often do students read expository texts? (biographies, personal narratives, newspaper and magazine articles, etc.)

☐ What types of literature do students read most frequently? (short stories, novels, poetry, plays, etc.)

☐ How familiar are students with alternative forms of text? (advertisements, Web sites, written directions, pamphlets, etc.)

☐ How often do students read texts written for different purposes? (to entertain, to inform, to express, to persuade, etc.)

☐ What literary devices can students identify? (point of view, flashback, symbolism, foreshadowing, mood, tone, style, suspense, dialogue, figurative language, etc.)

☐ Can students distinguish between the author's point of view and the author's purpose?

☐ What story elements can students identify? (plot, setting, character, conflict, resolution, theme, etc.)

☐ Can students analyze character, including traits, motivations, conflicts (both internal and external), points of view, transitions, and changes?

☐ How often do students use context clues to determine meanings of words?

Writing Questions

☐ How often do students use graphic organizers before writing?

☐ How often do students write in response to a text they have read?

☐ What are the most common forms of writing done by students?

☐ Do students have experience using a basic essay format?

☐ What forms of essay writing can students do? (persuasive, descriptive, process, comparison/contrast, etc.)

☐ How often do students use evidence from a text to support their opinions?

☐ How often do students revise their writing or use authentic writing to identify errors in grammar, sentence construction, and basic meaning?

☐ How often do students use dictionaries or thesauruses during the writing process?

☐ How often do students use literary devices in their own writing?

☐ How often do students use their own experiences in their writing?

For a tailor-made checklist based on your state's standards, see the information provided by your state's education department or agency on the language arts standards for grade seven. The Web site addresses at the end of Chapter 1 (pages 8–12) should provide links to lists of standards available on-line.

Diagnostic Reading Test—Grade 7

Directions: Read the article. Then, answer questions 1 through 6 on your answer sheet.

Fly Away Home

(1) Danny Lopez feeds his pet, Cosmo, lots of fats, carbohydrates, and proteins for many weeks. Then he takes Cosmo several hundred miles away from home, lets him out of his carrier, and leaves him there to find his way back home without help. No, this is not some episode of a new reality show about the true lives of forgotten pets. Danny Lopez and lots of other racers train their pet homing pigeons to race competitively by using their innate ability to fly back to their original coops.

(2) Pigeon racing is a historical and technical sport spreading its wings in parts of the East Coast and other regions in the country. Using homing pigeons, racers train their birds to fly up to 500 miles from distant locations back "home"—their lofts on rooftops throughout more cities than you might realize. The competition is based on speed and navigation; the bird who can navigate more accurately and thus fly at a faster rate of speed back to its destination is the winner, not necessarily the bird who gets home first. The winning birds can garner several thousand dollars for their owners depending on the particular race.

(3) But just in case you're thinking any old pigeon will do, wait a second before trying to catch your own Cosmo in the park. The homing pigeon is a specifically bred variety of pigeon, not at all like those living in parks and other urban settings. This breed of pigeon is able to use several sources of information to help it find its way back to its nesting place, without the help of its owner or other technology. Although no one knows conclusively what these pigeons use as their internal tracking system, experts say it is a combination of things: the position of the sun, the earth's magnetic field, and even their own senses.

(4) Since homing pigeons are such a unique breed, they can be very pricey pets. Some new birds can cost as much as $100,000! Birds with this kind of price tag are pedigreed, coming from crossings of varieties that are trained racers. These birds are born to race, flying at speeds up to 60 miles an hour. Living up to their name, they will fly without stopping for rest or food when set free to find their way home.

GO ON

(5) Although it may seem like a new cutting-edge sport, pigeon racing has a long history. Using birds to send messages has been done for centuries, starting as far back as the 12th century. In the 1800s, the activity evolved into an international sport. Today, races are held all over the country, organized within race seasons and specific racing clubs. In the late summer and early fall, young birds (birds hatched during that calendar year) are raced separately from more mature ones, flying shorter distances of 100 to 300 miles. Races for mature birds are held in the spring and early summer, and can range from 100 up to 600 miles.

(6) How the birds navigate may be one of nature's mysteries, but how the races are organized is no secret, and has been structured into an exact science. The process begins with the bird racers, who form a local club in their area. These clubs will decide upon the races they'll have within a season, including the distance, drop-off location, and potential prizes for the winners. Then, before the upcoming race season, precise measurements are taken from the chosen drop-off location to each racer's loft. Since each bird may be flying a slightly different distance, this detail becomes a major factor in the race. For example, in a 500-mile race, Cosmo may actually have to fly 502.5 miles to reach home, whereas a competitor may only have to fly 500.3 miles to get to its loft. Even if Cosmo doesn't get home first, he may still be the winner, depending on his rate of speed in combination with the total distance flown.

(7) Birds entered in races wear countermarks attached to the legs which act like flight speedometers. Before the race begins, owners provide a racing clock which will be used to house the countermark when the bird arrives home. These clocks are set to a universal time and then sealed. Once the birds arrive home, the owners remove the countermarks, place them in the clocks, and the exact arrival time is recorded. Once all the birds have returned, the clocks are opened by race officials and a winner is determined.

(8) You might be thinking that pigeon racing is an expensive hobby, but that's not necessarily so. You, too, can be a bird fancier. Although these birds can be costly to buy, some fanciers will give away young birds to those new to the sport. Depending on the pigeon clubs in your area, you may have a chance to race a bird sooner and more easily than you realize. Above all else, pigeon racers have a real love for the sport and are interested in helping those who want to explore it.

GO ON

1 Read this sentence from the passage.

> **Danny Lopez and lots of other racers train their pet homing pigeons to race competitively by using their innate ability to fly back to their original coops.**

What does the word **innate** mean?

A extra

B unusual

C natural

D strange

2 The sport of pigeon racing began—

F in the 15th century.

G in the 1800s.

H during the last 20 years.

J on the East Coast.

3 According to the article, young birds can race distances of up to—

A 100 miles.

B 300 miles.

C 500 miles.

D 600 miles.

4 Paragraph 6 is important because it—

F explains how birds are trained for a race.

G describes how homing pigeons navigate.

H explains how races are organized.

J tells about the history of the sport.

5 Based on information in the article, the reader can conclude that—

A although pigeon racing is an involved sport, it can be exciting and rewarding.

B pigeon racing can only be done in one region of the country.

C racing pigeons will soon become as popular as other forms of racing.

D pigeon racing is a new sport.

6 What is the author's attitude toward the subject of the article?

F negative

G hopeful

H positive

J doubtful

Diagnostic Reading Test—Grade 7 (continued)

Directions: Read the article. Then, answer questions 7 through 10 on your answer sheet.

Victoria Falls

(1)   Victoria Falls is located on the border of Zambia and Zimbabwe in the southeastern part of the African Continent. It is the largest waterfall in the world. It was created when the Zambezi River eroded away the softer rock between seams of hard, volcanic rock. Victoria Falls spans the width of the river at one of its widest points—it is over one mile in width. It is 355 feet tall, and the water plunges straight down. On average, 33,000 cubic feet of water pass over the falls per second.

(2)   Victoria Falls is about halfway through the over 1,600 miles of the Zambezi River. The water approaches the falls peacefully, but at the falls itself, the river's course becomes quite dramatic. First, the river drops into a chasm. Then it passes through a gorge only 210 feet wide and less than 400 feet long. From there, it gushes out wildly into a large pool called the Boiling Point, named for the massive amounts of mist that the turbulent water generates. The river then moves through a series of gorges, rapids, and man-made lakes before emptying into the Indian Ocean.

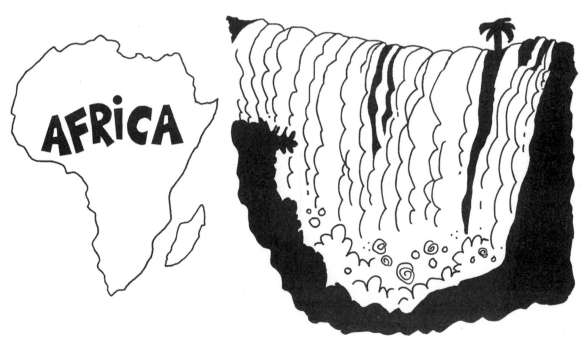

GO ON

7 According to the passage, which of the following is NOT true of Victoria Falls?

   A It is one of the most dramatic parts of the Zambezi River.

   B It is bigger than Niagara Falls.

   C It is big but it doesn't have a lot of water flowing over it.

   D It is in Africa.

8 Which word BEST describes the author's attitude toward Victoria Falls?

   F impressed

   G objective

   H impassive

   J overwhelmed

9 Which of the following phrases gives the BEST clue as to the meaning of the word **turbulent** in paragraph 2?

   A "gushes out wildly"

   B "mist"

   C "massive amounts"

   D "large pool"

10 Which of the following happens immediately after the Zambezi River reaches the Boiling Point pool?

   F The river drops 355 feet into a narrow chasm.

   G The river empties into the Indian Ocean.

   H The river approaches Victoria Falls.

   J The river flows through a series of gorges, rapids, and man-made lakes.

GO ON ➡

Diagnostic Reading Test—Grade 7 (continued)

Directions: Read the story. Then, answer questions 11 through 16 on your answer sheet.

The Perfect Present

(1) Lynn looked at the calendar, and suddenly realized that her father's birthday was only a few days away. She had been saving her baby-sitting money for a birthday present, but still needed twenty more dollars to buy him the golf club he wanted from the pro shop downtown. "What am I going to do?" Lynn thought to herself.

(2) Lynn's mother had just walked into the kitchen when she saw Lynn looking perplexed. "What's the matter, Lynn?" her mother asked.

(3) "Mom, I don't know how I'll be able to get Dad that golf club he's been talking about for his birthday. I wanted to surprise him, but I won't have enough money saved in time. I have to get him something!" Lynn's voice quivered as if she were about to cry.

(4) Lynn's mother put her arm around Lynn and said gently, "I have to run a few errands. Why don't you come with me? Besides, your father's present can wait."

(5) Lynn and her mother drove to the shopping center where her mother had to run her errands. "Lynn, I'm going to return a few things at this clothing store, and then get some groceries. Do you want to tag along or go window shopping? There's a new pet store down on the corner. They advertised having lots of unusual animals. Maybe you can find something there for your father."

(6) Lynn was still feeling glum about her father's present, and shrugged her shoulders. "Well, I guess I'll just wander around the shops," she replied. "I'll wait for you down at the pet store."

(7) "Sounds like a plan," her mother winked back.

(8) Lynn meandered in and out of the shops, browsing for potential gifts. "None of these things seems special enough," Lynn thought to herself. Finally she made her way to the pet store. Posted in the windows were signs that read, "Find the perfect gift at Perfect Pets!" Walking into the store, Lynn saw the biggest variety of animals she had ever seen in one place. While playing with some kittens in a playpen, Lynn browsed among the other cages full of iguanas, parrots, rabbits, and tanks of tropical fish.

(9) Then, just as she was about to leave to find her mother, she heard a funny high-pitched squeak from the back of the store.

GO ON

(10) "What's that?" Lynn thought out loud.

(11) "That's an Abyssinian guinea pig," responded one of the store clerks. "They love people and make great pets. Want to hold one?" From the look on her face, the clerk could tell that Lynn was hesitant. "I was just going to give him a carrot. Here, why don't you feed him." Handing Lynn a fresh carrot, she gestured for Lynn to follow her to the guinea pig's cage.

(12) Once Lynn saw the little furry shape, she couldn't help but giggle. It had short hair on its face, but the rest of its body was covered with longer hair that stuck out in all directions, like a fluffy fountain of water. Over one of its eyes was a large brown spot. The guinea pig seemed to smile when it saw Lynn with the carrot in her hand and squeaked so loudly that Lynn smiled back.

(13) "Is this the only one you have?" Lynn asked.

(14) "Yes. We've sold all the others. I think he's a little lonely without any company," said the clerk.

(15) Lynn picked up the guinea pig and fed him the carrot. The furry little animal munched happily on the treat. Stroking the guinea pig, Lynn started thinking about whether or not her father would like an animal for a present. "He loves animals, but maybe guinea pigs are too hard to care for," thought Lynn. "Who knows if he would even think a guinea pig was cute?"

(16) Just as Lynn placed the little animal back in its cage, she felt a hand on her shoulder. "Lynn, it looks as if you found a new friend," said her mother.

(17) "Mom, this is an Abyssinian guinea pig. Isn't he cute? I had a crazy thought that Dad might like him, but I don't know. I mean, Dad is probably too busy to take care of a guinea pig," replied Lynn.

(18) Lynn's mother smiled and said, "Well, did you know that when your father was growing up, he raised guinea pigs? He had a male and female that had lots of litters. When the babies were big enough, he would sell them to neighbors and the local pet store."

(19) "Wow! Then do you think he might like another one now as a pet?" asked Lynn with a look of anticipation on her face.

(20) "Lynn, I think giving your father a new pet is the perfect present," her mother responded. "Plus, taking care of this little guy is something you could do together." Lynn couldn't wait to get home and give her father his birthday present a few days early.

GO ON

Diagnostic Reading Test—Grade 7 (continued)

11 At first, Lynn doesn't want to consider giving a pet as a gift because—

   A she has a different gift in mind for her father.

   B she knows her father doesn't like small animals.

   C she doesn't have enough money to buy one.

   D her father already had a guinea pig as a pet.

12 What is paragraph 12 mainly about?

   F a conversation between Lynn and her mother

   G a description of how Lynn feeds the guinea pig

   H a description of the guinea pig that Lynn finds

   J a conversation between Lynn and the store clerk

13 Which words help the reader understand the meaning of the word **glum** in paragraph 6?

   A "father" and "something"

   B "wander" and "still"

   C "feeling" and "shrugged"

   D "shoulders" and "present"

14 Which sentence from the passage indicates a change in Lynn's attitude?

   F Lynn started thinking whether or not her father would like an animal for a present.

   G Lynn's voice quivered as if she were about to cry.

   H "None of these things seem special enough," Lynn thought to herself.

   J From the look on her face, the clerk could tell that Lynn was hesitant.

15 What does the word **meandered** mean in paragraph 8?

   A was lost

   B grumbled

   C wandered

   D looked

16 SHORT ANSWER: On your answer sheet, please answer the following question in complete sentences.

Reread the last sentence in the story. What do you think will happen next? Support your conclusion with evidence from the text.

END OF PRACTICE TEST

Diagnostic Reading Test—Grade 7
Answer Sheet

Directions: Record your answers on this answer sheet. Be sure to fill in each bubble completely and erase any stray marks. Use the lines provided to write the short-answer response.

1 Ⓐ Ⓑ Ⓒ Ⓓ

2 Ⓕ Ⓖ Ⓗ Ⓙ

3 Ⓐ Ⓑ Ⓒ Ⓓ

4 Ⓕ Ⓖ Ⓗ Ⓙ

5 Ⓐ Ⓑ Ⓒ Ⓓ

6 Ⓕ Ⓖ Ⓗ Ⓙ

7 Ⓐ Ⓑ Ⓒ Ⓓ

8 Ⓕ Ⓖ Ⓗ Ⓙ

9 Ⓐ Ⓑ Ⓒ Ⓓ

10 Ⓕ Ⓖ Ⓗ Ⓙ

11 Ⓐ Ⓑ Ⓒ Ⓓ

12 Ⓕ Ⓖ Ⓗ Ⓙ

13 Ⓐ Ⓑ Ⓒ Ⓓ

14 Ⓕ Ⓖ Ⓗ Ⓙ

15 Ⓐ Ⓑ Ⓒ Ⓓ

16 SHORT ANSWER: Use the space below to answer the question in complete sentences.

Reread the last sentence in the story. What do you think will happen next? Support your conclusion with evidence from the text.

_____

_____

_____

_____

_____

_____

_____

_____

_____

Test-Taking Skills and Strategies

When preparing for a test, students don't normally prepare for *how* to take the test. They are usually more worried about what they do or do not know than about how their approach can affect their performance. And with the added pressure of today's high-stakes assessment tests, the concept of strategic test taking may be the last thing on students' minds.

As your students' testing coach, your role is thus twofold: to give students the knowledge they need to do well on the tests and to equip them with strategies they can use to refuel, relax, or refocus in order to reach the finish line. This chapter outlines several strategies students can apply to problems that may surface when taking tests.

Getting students into the right frame of mind for testing is one of the most challenging tasks facing a coach. This chapter addresses the most common issues involving testing and offers both you and your students ways to incorporate test-taking skills and strategies into the framework of test preparation. The chapter is broken down into the following sections:

- ✗ Reducing Test Anxiety
- ✗ Pacing
- ✗ Strategic Guessing
- ✗ Reading Strategies
- ✗ Writing Strategies
- ✗ Before the Test

The boxed "Coaching Clues" that appear throughout this chapter offer suggestions for additional practice or related activities. Some activities have accompanying reproducible handouts. These reproducible pages are arranged by strategy beginning on page 42.

Reducing Test Anxiety

When faced with standardized tests, students may experience a range of reactions, including anxiety. To help students replace test anxiety with confidence, talk about the tests, familiarize students with the test format and structure, and give them techniques to deal with any stress or distractions that may occur during testing.

You may want to begin by asking students to reflect on their own attitudes toward tests. Discuss the different feelings the prospect of taking a test may arouse, as well as how students might deal with those feelings. Ask students to share any strategies they may already use when taking tests.

> ***Coaching Clue*** — Using the *Testing Questionnaire* reproducible (page 42) as a starting point, encourage students to discuss and reflect on the testing process.

The more familiar students are with the tests they will take, the less stress they will likely experience. One way to help reduce test anxiety is to make students so familiar with the test format that they don't even flinch when faced with the actual tests. Pages 30 and 31 include several ways to familiarize students with your state's assessment tests.

Break It Down

Take a sample, benchmark, or previously released test developed by your state's education department and break it down for analysis. Divide the class into small groups and ask each group to analyze the format, content, language, and style of the test. Once all of the groups have completed their analyses and shared their findings, review the major points about each aspect of the test. Make a chart or poster to display as a classroom reference.

> **Coaching Clue** — Use the *Meet Your Reading Test* reproducible (page 43) to try out this break-it-down strategy. Students can use the questions on the handout as a guide in their analysis and discussion.

Be a Copycat

Design assignments, quizzes, and tests in the same layout and format as your state's tests. If the reading test includes a variety of text structures, incorporate those same structures into any tests or projects in your curriculum. For example, if students are required to read everything from interviews to letters to the editor, have them rewrite story information in those formats, or test students on content using those types of text structures.

Test Experts

Have students write sample questions in the same format as your state's tests. The questions can be based on texts they are currently reading or on concepts they are learning in class. Have students test one another using their sample questions.

Tip Trade

Students may already have some tricks up their sleeves when it comes to dealing with testing issues. Before test time, have students brainstorm different tricks or hints they have for dealing with stress, pacing, guessing, or other test-taking issues. Then, have them teach these skills to one another in small groups or to the entire class. As a follow-up, give them opportunities to practice these new skills either with practice tests or tests written by the students themselves. (See "Test Experts" above.)

Make It Real

Common sense tells us that the more preparation we have before attempting something, the better we will do. In the same vein, testing experts state that the more exposure students have to the look, feel, and experience of tests before testing day, the better they will perform.

With this in mind, give students an authentic simulation of the testing experience at least once before the actual tests. You could use the sample tests included in Chapters 3 and 6, or sample tests from your state's education department. Alternatively, design your own test with the look and feel of your state's tests, but based on recent coursework learned by the students. Although you don't want to reach testing overload with students, you do want to give them opportunities to apply what they have learned. Creating authentic test simulations can help you and your students work out any kinks in the process while strengthening their skills and building their confidence.

Some schools even hold simulation days when students throughout the school take benchmark or trial tests. Use these simulations to promote discussion with your students about their test-taking experiences. Make sure students realize that a low score on a practice test is nothing to get worried or upset about. Instead, a low score should be seen as an excellent way to spot areas that still need improvement before the actual test.

Coaching Clue — After students have taken some practice quizzes and tests, have them analyze the test-taking experience. Use the *Talking It Over* reproducible (page 44) as a guide for this activity.

Pacing

While the majority of state standardized tests are timed, your own state's tests may not be. But regardless of time limits, pacing can play a key role in a student's testing success. Pacing can help students stay on track by helping them focus their concentration, maintain their stamina, and offset any anxiety.

To introduce the concept of pacing, have students envision the tests as a series of track-and-field events. Each part of the test is like a different event. Even if students want to get the best time or highest score for one event, pacing their energy and concentration among all the events they face will yield a better result overall. Have them practice and employ the following strategies to bolster their endurance and even out their tempo during testing.

X-O Strategy

A steady pace ensures the best performance. Sometimes, however, a student will come across a question that stumps him, causing him to lose his sense of rhythm. Most students approach questions as if they have to be done in order. When they hit hard questions, they get stuck and refuse to move on. And the longer they stay stuck, the more anxious and frustrated they become. This is a strategic mistake. Students' scores and attitudes will both get a boost if students make two or three passes through a test, each time skipping questions that seem too hard and going back to them after they have tried to answer all of the other questions.

The X-O strategy is a simple way to maintain a good pace and maximize scores. When working through a section, a student should first take the time to solve or answer any questions she can. However, if she starts to struggle with a confusing problem and spends more than a few minutes on it without coming up with an answer, she should stop and mark an "X" in the margin next to the question. This is a "maybe" question. The student could probably figure out the solution if she spent some more time, but for now she needs to move on and try to answer other easier problems.

If the student comes to a question that initially makes no sense to her at all, she should mark an "O" in the margin. This is a "guessing" question. Using strategic guessing techniques can help improve the odds of the student selecting the correct answer on this type of question.

After the student has answered every question she can, she should return to the X questions first and try them again. If they still give her trouble, she should apply strategic guessing techniques, such as process of elimination (discussed on pages 34–35), to eliminate any incorrect answers. Once some of the answer choices have been eliminated, the student can make an educated guess. After the student has tried to answer all of the X questions, she should go back to the O questions and apply the same strategic guessing techniques.

The X-O strategy keeps students from freezing up when faced with tough questions. It also encourages them to answer every question, which will ultimately help their scores.

> ***Coaching Clue*** — For practice using the X-O strategy with students, see the *X-O Strategy* reproducible (page 45) at the end of this chapter.

Time-Outs

Most experts believe that the average person can only handle 45 minutes of learning new material before reaching complete absorption. This belief is the reasoning behind the "45/15 rule": after 45 minutes of study, take a 15-minute break. If this is a good method for students to use when studying, why not apply it, in a modified form, to taking a test? Tell students that one way to pace themselves during a test is to take a time-out after each section. Alternatively, they can take a break every half hour or so, stretching a bit while still at their desks. Encourage students to use the timed breaks to get up and stretch, get a drink of water, or walk around the hall a bit to refresh themselves before going back to the test.

Desk Stretches

Most state assessment tests are several hours long. Students understandably find it difficult and uncomfortable to remain in the same position for a very long time. To help students combat desk fatigue, teach them some stretches they can do while sitting at their desks. The exercises that follow on page 33 are written so that you can read them directly from the page to your students.

Four-Square Neck Stretches

1. Sitting straight in your chair, tilt your head forward. Try to touch your chin to your chest. Hold for five counts.

2. Tilt your head backward and look up at the ceiling. Let the back of your head rest on the base of your neck while keeping your shoulders relaxed. Hold for five counts.

3. Tilt your head to the right, bringing your ear close to your right shoulder. Hold for five counts.

4. Tilt your head to the left, bringing your ear close to your left shoulder. Hold for five counts.

Shoulder Roll and Pull

1. While seated at your desk, roll both shoulders forward in a circular motion. Continue for a count of ten. Try to keep your neck relaxed. Concentrate on rotating your shoulders in circles rather than just lifting them straight up and down.

2. Switch direction and roll your shoulders backward, also for a count of ten.

3. Next, clasp your hands together and extend your arms out from your chest, as if you are getting ready to hit a volleyball with your forearms. Concentrate on separating your shoulder blades, pulling the muscles in your upper back away from the center and out toward your hands. Hold for five counts.

Answer Bubbles

Nearly all standardized tests require students to record their answers by filling in some form of lettered bubbles. As with anything else, the more experience students have using bubble answer sheets, the more natural the process will feel during the actual tests. Give students the practice they need by incorporating bubble-style answer grids into everyday activities, from daily warm-ups to homework review or pop quizzes.

One of the pitfalls of skipping a question in the test booklet is that a student may forget to skip that problem on the answer sheet. Having students use simple bookmarks or rulers while testing can help them stay on top of which problems they are skipping and need to go back to later. Check your state's guidelines to see if tools like these are allowed during testing.

Another approach is to have students record their choices on the answer sheet after they have finished each section. This reduces the risk of filling in the bubbles incorrectly. Just tell students to write or circle their final answer choice for each question in the test booklet itself. Then, after each section, they can transfer their answers to the answer sheet.

Coaching Clue — To give students extra practice, provide bubble grids similar to those on your state's tests for students to use with short quizzes or other classroom assignments.

Strategic Guessing

Even though state assessment exams do not normally feature a guessing penalty, this does not mean students should just guess randomly. Encourage students to use strategic guessing strategies by explaining how this can help them choose smart answers and, in turn, raise their scores.

Make it clear to your students from the start that guessing is not cheating. Even if students think they couldn't possibly know the right answer, remind them that they have multiple tools on hand for every question. They can use prior knowledge and experience, as well as what they just learned by reading a passage. These tools, combined with smart guessing, can all help a student figure out what the correct answer might be.

Although the X-O strategy (pages 31–32) can help students pace themselves throughout the test, it can also be used as the first step toward guessing strategically. If students begin by answering the questions they definitely know first, they can then go back and deal with the remaining questions using smart guessing and the process of elimination.

POE: Process of Elimination

Applying POE, or the process of elimination, during a test simply means weeding out any unsuitable answer choices. The inherent beauty of multiple-choice tests is that the correct answers are always provided—students just have to learn how to identify them.

Students are often amazed and encouraged when you explain that the right answers are in plain view in their test booklets. To get students comfortable with POE, first explain that the answers are all there on the page. Then, show them how the process works. Write a sample question and answer choices, such as the following, on the board or on an overhead transparency:

How high is Mount Everest?

      A   528 feet
      B   29,035 feet
      C   1,263,328 feet
      D   1,480 feet

Tell your students that with some basic knowledge, good estimations, and common sense, they can reason through this question. Help them work through the POE process. First, talk about Mount Everest. What is it? A really tall mountain. What else do they know about it? They might know that people try to climb it but don't always succeed, even after many days of trying. This should give students some idea of the distance from the foot of the mountain to its peak. Next, help your students generate some lengths and heights to use for reference. For example, how long is a football field? Many students will know that a football field is 100 yards long, which is 300 feet. And how long is a mile? Some students will know this, too—5,280 feet. Ask them to think about how high a mountain might be, and then consider the answer choices.

- Choice A (528 feet) is less than twice the length of a football field. It would hardly be the height of a respectable mountain. Choice A can be eliminated.

- Choice B (29,035 feet) sounds like a lot. That would be about six miles of mountain. Choice B could be right, but keep going.

- Choice C (1,263,328 feet) sounds impressive, but does it make sense? A mountain that high would be about 240 miles tall. Many states aren't even 240 miles wide. Mountains just aren't that tall.

- Choice D (1,480 feet), like Choice A, just does not seem tall enough. It is less than one mile. That leaves Choice B, which is correct.

Point out to students that even though they did not actually know the height of Mount Everest, they were able to make a good guess by eliminating obviously wrong answers. This kind of reasoning can be applied to many standardized test questions with excellent results.

> ***Coaching Clue*** — To try this as an exercise with students, tailor the steps outlined above to address a sample question from one of your state's practice tests.

Critical Words and POE

As they apply the steps of POE, advise students to look for any critical (or extreme) words in the questions or answer choices. These words, which are often underlined, italicized, bold-faced, or set in all caps, may help students narrow down their choices or guide them in the right direction. Have students circle or underline any extreme words, such as:

NEVER	ONLY	ANY
EXCEPT	BEST	ALL
ALWAYS	NOT	NONE

Explain how these words can help students eliminate answer choices when common sense and prior experience are not helping. Very often, though not always, answer choices with critical, or extreme, words in them are wrong. If a student is forced to guess, you can advise her to cross out choices that involve critical or extreme words.

Flip a Coin

If a student has narrowed down the answer options as much as possible by eliminating wrong or unlikely choices, but he still has two or three possible answers, he should just pick an answer—guess and move on. The odds are that over the course of the test he will guess correctly at least some of the time, thus improving his score. However, completely random guessing should be discouraged. It gives students the feeling that they can just give up and guess on hard questions when, in fact, a little POE and deductive reasoning could help them get close to the right answers. The fact is, unless there is a guessing penalty on your state's test, students have nothing to lose by guessing. Tell them to answer every question but to guess blindly only if they have exhausted all of their smart guessing strategies.

Reading Strategies

Reading for a Purpose

Explain to students that before they read anything, it is important to determine why they are reading it. For example, are they reading to get information, to be entertained, to learn something, or to explore another side of an issue? When students look at a text, they may not consciously think about why they are going to read it, beyond the fact that it is something they *have* to read. To ensure greater comprehension and better results when having to answer questions about a text, tell students to keep a purpose in mind when reading.

Questions, Questions

If students are familiar with the different types of questions they may encounter on a test, they will likely be better able to answer them. Review and explain the most familiar types of questions well in advance of the real tests. Reading questions can generally be organized into three categories: Instant Recall, Pause and Look, and Reader and Passage.

Instant Recall — This type of question asks students to recall information directly from the text, usually in a specific place. Example: "What color was Jennifer's balloon?"

Pause and Look — This type of question asks students to pause after reading, think back on what they read, and look for related information in the passage. The answer may not be found in one specific place in the text, but rather in a combination of details. Example: "How are the king and the servant different?"

Reader and Passage — This type of question asks students to apply what they already know to what they have just read in the passage. Reader and Passage questions are the most challenging because they involve higher-level thinking skills, such as making inferences, drawing conclusions, or making comparisons. Example: "How did Jake feel when his dog was stolen?"

Identifying Text Structures

Students can also use text structure to help them find answers to questions. If students understand how a text is organized, they can focus on looking in a particular part of the text to answer each question most efficiently. For example, the basic structure of a story includes a beginning, a middle, and an end. The setting, characters, and other essential details are usually introduced to the reader at the beginning of a story. If a question following the passage asks for the name of a character or where the story takes place, students should know (based on the text's structure) to look for clues in the beginning of the story. If, on the other hand, there is a question about a problem or conflict, students should know that the details will probably be found somewhere in the middle of the story.

KWL Charts and Other Graphic Organizers

KWL charts are a great way to accustom students to using graphic organizers to help them understand reading passages. KWL is a somewhat awkwardly constructed abbreviation for "What I Already <u>K</u>now," "What I <u>W</u>ant to Learn," and "What I <u>L</u>earned." The more often students incorporate what they already know with what they learn while reading, the more likely they are to better answer questions that ask them to make inferences, compare and contrast, identify author's purpose or point of view, or draw conclusions.

Here is a very simple example of a KWL chart:

K What I Already <u>K</u>now	W What I <u>W</u>ant to Learn	L What I <u>L</u>earned
Platypuses are mammals that lay eggs.	What does the word *platypus* mean?	*Platypus* comes from Greek and means "flat-footed."

Many reading tests ask students to complete graphic organizers with information from a text. The types of organizers are similar to those used to help students organize their ideas before writing. Some of the most common types of organizers students may be asked to complete include:

- ✘ Venn diagrams or compare/contrast charts
- ✘ Clustering organizers like webs or brainstorming charts
- ✘ Sequence maps or chain-of-events flowcharts
- ✘ Story maps

One of the best ways to prepare students for dealing with graphic organizers is to use them frequently in class, interchanging the types used with a variety of text structures. For example, a cluster or webbing diagram could be used for a nonfiction passage on dolphins, as well as to show the attributes or choices of a character from a story. When reading stories in class, have students compare two characters by completing a Venn diagram or a compare/contrast chart.

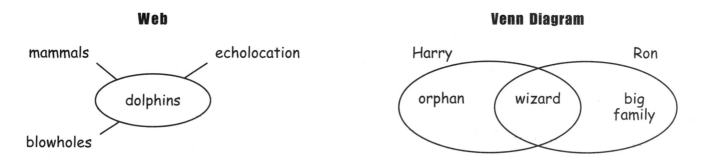

Modified SQ3R

Many teachers know SQ3R as an effective technique for retaining and comprehending reading material, but it can also be applied to test taking. Students can use an adaptation of this method when dealing with reading selections on standardized tests. This modified strategy can be used with novels, textbooks, and expository texts, as well as short stories and other narrative passages. Teach students to apply this modified version of SQ3R when approaching a reading selection and related questions on a test: Skim, Question, Read, Respond and Review.

SKIM the passage before reading:

X   Look at the title. What does it tell you about the selection?

X   Look at any illustrations, photos, graphs, or maps.

X   Skim through the questions before reading the passage.

Note: Some may argue that skimming can cause students to miss out on the subtleties of what the questions are really asking—students may simply look for the answers rather than reading the whole passage. Familiarizing themselves with the questions first, however, can help students focus on what the reading passage may be about. If students read the passage from beginning to end with the questions already in mind, it is similar to having a teacher provide them with a study guide of ideas, questions, or concepts to guide the reading they do in class.

QUESTION while skimming:

X   Turn the title into a question to help get you interested in the subject. For example, if the title is "An Ancient Disk's Secret Message," change it into a question to focus your reading: "What is the ancient disk's secret message?"

X   Think about what you already know about words in the title or the subject of the passage. Connect your own knowledge and experience with the text as you skim.

Note: Part of examining the title is to get students thinking about what they already know about the subject of the selection. If students are not sure what the passage is about, they can look at the words they do understand in the title and in the title question. What does the word *ancient* mean? What does the phrase *secret message* bring to mind? When might a secret message have been used? Could this be an old form of messaging? Was it an earlier version of a computer disk—an ancient disk?

READ the passage actively

X   Read with a purpose. Based on the title and other clues gleaned from skimming the passage, why are you going to read it? Why did the author write it in the first place? The major purposes are to inform, entertain, persuade, and express.

X   Read carefully and at a comfortable pace, thinking about the questions, what you already know about the subject, and any new information you discover.

X   Mark up the text. As you read, underline phrases that stand out, that make you think about something, or that might relate to one of the questions. Circle words you don't know or that you think are important. Write your comments, questions, or ideas about the reading in the margins of the text.

RESPOND and REVIEW

X   Read through the questions, answering the easiest ones first. Remember to use the X-O strategy for questions you can't answer right away.

X   Circle or underline any critical words in the questions and answer choices. Paraphrase each question by saying to yourself, "I'm actually looking for . . ."

X   Use the process of elimination to eliminate any answer choices you know are wrong. Cross out any choices that you know are not right, and then reread the choices that are left. Try to narrow it down to no more than two choices for each question.

X   Make an educated guess between the two answer choices that remain. If necessary, reread the passage for any clues or ideas about the answer.

Coaching Clue — Use the *Modified SQ3R* reproducible (page 46) as a reference when coaching students in this strategy.

Writing Strategies

Some states have writing tests at all grade levels while others test alternating grades (grades 5 and 7, or grades 6 and 8, for example). Check with your state's education department or agency to determine if your seventh graders will be asked to take a writing test.

Knowing How to Respond

One key strategy in writing an effective response to a writing prompt is determining what type of response to write. Although this may seem pretty straightforward, it is crucial that students understand the meanings of various writing terms as they plan their responses.

Coaching Clue — Use the *Writing Terms Chart* reproducibles (page 47) to review the key descriptors your students may see in writing prompts at the seventh-grade level.

Graphic Organizers

Using graphic organizers is a great way for students to organize their thoughts during the prewriting process. The following kinds of graphic organizers are particularly helpful in dealing with the types of writing prompts students are likely to encounter on standardized tests:

- ✗ KWL charts
- ✗ Venn diagrams or comparison/contrast charts
- ✗ Basic essay charts (for a five-paragraph essay with an introduction, three supporting evidence/body paragraphs, and a conclusion)
- ✗ Clustering organizers such as webs or brainstorming charts
- ✗ Sequence maps or chain-of-events flow charts
- ✗ Story maps

ROW Strategy

Preparing students for the writing portion of standardized tests simply means preparing them to express their thoughts in written form, since writing is actually thinking on paper. To help your students think before they write, have them follow the ROW strategy: Read/Rephrase, Organize, and Write.

Read/Rephrase — Read the prompt, circling or underlining any key words and phrases, such as *describe*, *compare and contrast*, *explain*, or *support*. Rephrase the prompt into another sentence that makes it clearer or easier to understand. Think of the purpose for writing and what structure to use.

Organize — Use a graphic organizer to organize your thoughts, evidence from the text, or examples from your own experiences to use while writing. Back up your points with specific information or quotations from the reading and/or examples from your own experience and include that on the organizer.

Write — Using the graphic organizer as a guide, write your response or essay.

Before the Test

The weeks before testing are perfect for reminding students that they are ready to handle whatever comes their way. It is also a great time for getting them excited about doing well on the tests. Here are two suggestions for pumping students up for testing:

✗ Hold a pep rally in your classroom. Students can write cheers, give pep talks, and make signs and banners to hang in the classroom for motivation.

✗ Have a T-shirt design contest, where students come up with a logo or graphic and a slogan. Organize a fundraiser to get the shirts made for students to wear during the tests.

Top Five Test-Taking Tips

Finally, give students these five tips to remember before, during, and after the test. You may want to enlarge this list, or rewrite it in your own words and post the list in the room where students will take their tests.

1. **Be confident!**
   Remember that you are prepped to do well. You have been "working out" to get ready for the tests and can succeed. It's time to show what you can do.

2. **Be prepared!**
   Get a good night's sleep, eat a hearty breakfast, and wear clothes suitable for testing—comfortable layers you can take off or put on in case the testing room is too hot or cold. Bring all of the materials you will need, such as pencils and a dictionary.

3. **Review the test before you begin.**
   Before you start, spend a few minutes reviewing the test carefully. Familiarize yourself with each section and then decide how to pace yourself.

4. **Be focused and relaxed.**
   To keep up your concentration, use the test-taking strategies you have learned. If you begin to feel tense, take a few deep breaths and do some stretches to relax.

5. **Look over the test when you are finished.**
   Make sure you have not skipped any sections and that you have answered every question. Check your answer sheet to make sure the bubbles are filled in neatly and correctly. Proofread any writing for proper spelling, grammar, and punctuation.

Testing Questionnaire

Directions: Read each statement. Mark your answer by checking the appropriate box.

ALWAYS	SOME OF THE TIME	NEVER	
☐	☐	☐	1. When I take a test, I feel confident that I am prepared and will do well.
☐	☐	☐	2. The night before a test, I get a good night's sleep.
☐	☐	☐	3. The morning before a test, I eat a good breakfast.
☐	☐	☐	4. During a test, I feel my mind racing.
☐	☐	☐	5. During a test, I feel alert and clearheaded.
☐	☐	☐	6. When taking a test, I forget what I have learned and then remember it after I'm finished.
☐	☐	☐	7. I make careless mistakes when taking a test.
☐	☐	☐	8. I check my work and my answers before I turn in a test.
☐	☐	☐	9. I rush to finish when I take a test.
☐	☐	☐	10. When taking a test, I overanalyze questions, change my answers a lot, or don't answer at all.
☐	☐	☐	11. If I don't know an answer, I narrow down my choices and take a guess.
☐	☐	☐	12. If I don't know an answer, I skip it and come back to it later.
☐	☐	☐	13. During a test, my breathing gets weird or my body feels tense.
☐	☐	☐	14. If I don't understand a question or what I'm supposed to do on a test, I ask for help.
☐	☐	☐	15. I lose concentration and am easily distracted by other people when taking a test.

Directions: Discuss your answers for numbers 1–15 with the rest of the class. Then, read each statement below. Mark your answer by checking the box for TRUE or FALSE.

☐ TRUE ☐ FALSE 16. It is better to guess on a question than to leave it blank.

☐ TRUE ☐ FALSE 17. Being the first one to finish a test is better than being the last one.

☐ TRUE ☐ FALSE 18. If you get bored or can't concentrate, you should just put your head down and go to sleep.

☐ TRUE ☐ FALSE 19. It's a waste of time to check your work before turning in a test.

☐ TRUE ☐ FALSE 20. You should never take a break during a test.

Meet Your Reading Test

Directions: Use the following questions as a guide to analyze your state's reading test. Be prepared to discuss your findings with the rest of the class.

1. Are there certain directions that are repeated throughout the test? If so, list them here.

   _____

   _____

   Are there any key words in these directions? If so, list them here. _____

   _____

2. Is there room to write, make notes, or underline words in the test booklet? _____
3. How many reading selections are there in all? _____
4. How long is each selection? _____
5. How are the reading selections organized on the pages? _____
6. Are any words in the reading selection *italicized*, underlined, or **boldfaced**? _____

   If so, what kinds of words are they? _____

7. What are the reading selections about? _____
8. What graphics are included? (photos, illustrations, charts, maps, etc.) _____

   _____

9. How many questions follow each selection? _____

   What types of questions are they? (multiple choice, short response, essay, etc.) _____

   _____

10. Are there any critical words in the questions, such as BEST, NOT, or EXCEPT? _____

    If so, list them here. _____

11. What concepts do the questions cover? (main idea, point of view, comprehension, details from the text, context clues, etc.)

    _____

12. After analyzing the reading selections and questions, what do you think you need to do in order to prepare for the test?

    _____

    _____

Talking It Over

Directions: Answer the questions in the chart below. Use your answers as a starting point to discuss your testing experiences.

Reflecting on the Tests	
What did you find the **most difficult** about the **reading** test?	What **techniques or strategies** did you use during the **reading** test?
What did you find the **most difficult** about the **writing** test?	What **techniques or strategies** did you use during the **writing** test?

Preparing for the Real Thing
List the **major skills you want to work on** as you prepare for the tests.

X-O Strategy

Directions: Use the X-O strategy to guide you through the test-taking process. Be sure to mark your test as instructed below and to complete all portions of this handout.

Round 1: Read through the questions on the test. As you read, answer all of the questions you can without too much effort or time. Mark those answers on your answer sheet.

A. Mark an X by each question that you think you can answer, but are not sure about. Record the number of questions marked with an X here: _____

B. Mark an O by each question for which you would have to guess the answer. Record the number of questions marked with an O here: _____

Round 2: Go back through the test and try to answer all of the questions marked with an X.

A. If you need to, reread or review any of the questions. Look for additional information to help you clarify anything or support the answers you think are correct.

B. Mark those answers on your answer sheet.

Round 3: Go back through the test and try to answer all of the questions marked with an O.

A. Note any critical words in the questions. Circle or underline these words and write them on the following lines:

_____

_____

B. Apply POE, or the process of elimination.

- Use common sense and logical reasoning to eliminate bad or unlikely answer choices. Think about how any critical words can help you determine the answer by eliminating some of the answer choices.

- Cross out any answer choices that you know are incorrect or unlikely.

- Try to narrow down the answer choices to two per question.

C. Use your own prior knowledge, information from the text, or any other clues given (such as captions or illustrations) to make educated guesses. Mark your answers on your answer sheet.

Modified SQ3R

SKIM – QUESTION – READ – RESPOND – REVIEW	
SKIM **before reading**	• Look at the title, headings, and subheadings. • Look at any pictures, charts, graphs, or maps. • Skim the questions to see what is being asked.
QUESTION **while skimming**	• Turn the title, headings, and subheadings into questions. • Think about what you already know about the subject. • Write down questions you have in the margins of the text or on a sheet of scratch paper.
READ the **passage actively**	• Read with a purpose. Think about the author's purpose for writing: to inform, entertain, express, or persuade. • Read the captions under any illustrations or graphics. • Mark any underlined, *italicized*, or **boldfaced** words and phrases. • Make notes and underline words, phrases, or sentences that relate to the questions. • Stop and reread any unclear or confusing paragraphs. • Try to get a sense of the main idea of each paragraph and of the passage as a whole.
RESPOND **and REVIEW**	• Answer questions based on what you read. • Reread where necessary. • Use strategies to help you answer the questions.

Writing Terms Chart

Term	Definition — What It Means
Compare	Look at the similarities between two or more things, characters, events, ideas, or problems. In your writing, emphasize the similarities, although comparing usually implies looking at the differences, too.
Contrast	Look at the differences between two or more things, characters, events, ideas, or problems. In your writing, emphasize the differences, although contrasting usually implies looking at the similarities, too.
Define	Clearly state what something is, like the definition in a dictionary or an encyclopedia. To support the definition, use examples or details from what you know, have read, or have experienced.
Describe	Paint a picture with words, giving details that relate to the senses: sight, smell, touch, taste, and hearing.
Discuss	Carefully examine all sides of the topic, presenting the pros and cons. This type of writing should be detailed and thoughtful.
Explain/ Express	Present the how, why, and what about the topic. Explain an opinion or a view by offering reasons and examples that help the reader understand.
Narrate (Write a story)	Use all of the major parts of a story: setting, characters, beginning action (introduction), rising action (middle), climax or conflict, and ending action (conclusion). Include details and literary elements to make the story interesting and related to the prompt.
Persuade	State your view or opinion on a topic. Defend and support your view with evidence (examples or reasons) to convince the reader to agree with you. In your writing, you should also discuss the opposing view or side in order to persuade the reader that your view makes more sense. You can appeal to the reader's emotions (emotional appeal) or logic (rational appeal).
Reflect	Look back at or reflect on your experiences, ideas, or reading and write about them, expressing what you learned in some way.
Summarize	Condense something down to the main points or essential facts. Describe the main ideas or events, and leave out all of the details.

Skill-Building Reading Activities

Becoming a better reader and writer is perhaps not a high personal priority for most students. Realistically, we know their thoughts may be more immediate, such as "When will class be over?" or "What's for lunch?" We all remember sitting in class diagramming sentences and wishing we were outside riding a bicycle instead.

As a teacher, you know that strong verbal skills are vital for students' success—not just because they will be tested on these skills, but because reading and writing are the foundations of most types of learning in school. This chapter includes 15 different activities designed to help you build and reinforce students' reading and writing skills. Each activity provides an engaging way for students to practice one or more key skills that will be assessed on your state's standardized tests. Students will be asked to use their knowledge, experience, and imagination. Each activity is structured in the following format:

- ✗ Skills/State Standards—breakdown of the skills addressed in the activity
- ✗ Description—brief summary of the activity
- ✗ Materials You Need—list of materials required for the activity
- ✗ Getting Ready—tips for the teacher and a description of what to do in order to prepare for the activity
- ✗ Introducing the Activity—suggestions for introducing the activity and capturing students' interest
- ✗ Modeling the Activity—ideas for demonstrating the activity (if applicable)
- ✗ Activity in Practice—step-by-step instructions for working through the activity
- ✗ Extensions—variations, extensions, and other teaching suggestions (if applicable)

All of the activities are designed to be hands-on and group-oriented, requiring active participation by your students. They are also flexible in nature, however, and can be modified to meet your students' needs as well as give students individual practice. You can use the activities in any order. You may find that some are better suited to the particular needs of your students than others.

Some activities also include reproducible pages. These pages are found at the end of this chapter, beginning on page 85.

The matrix on page 49 organizes the activities by the predominant skills or standards they address. Some activities address more than one skill and may, therefore, appear under more than one category on the chart.

Matrix of Skills Addressed in Reading Activities

Skill/State Standard	Activity	Page
Comprehension	Webmasters	50
Identifying main idea and supporting details	Literary Logos Third Eye	52 64
Summarizing and paraphrasing	Perfect Pitch You Don't Say! Tell It Like It Is	54 76 80
Analyzing character	Laundry Line Fortune-Teller	57 78
Story structure and elements	Webmasters Perfect Pitch	50 54
Identifying cause and effect	Perfect Pitch One Thing Leads to Another Cliff-Hanger	54 62 66
Comparing and contrasting	Textual Duo Tell It Like It Is	60 80
Understanding sequence and chronology	Perfect Pitch One Thing Leads to Another	54 62
Making predictions	Third Eye Cliff-Hanger Fortune-Teller	64 66 78
Making inferences and drawing conclusions	The Great Debate	68
Distinguishing fact from opinion	Fact-Checker Challenge Tell Me about It	74 82
Using context clues	Got Your Back	71
Using graphic organizers	One Thing Leads to Another	62
Understanding the author's purpose	Tell Me about It	82
Identifying the author's perspective	Fact-Checker Challenge Tell Me about It	74 82

Webmasters

Description

Students today are pretty savvy when it comes to surfing the Web or playing computer games. This activity will capitalize on students' exposure to and knowledge of the Internet to help them work on comprehension, story structure, and interpretation skills. As Webmasters, students will demonstrate their understanding of a story by creating simple

Web sites that incorporate each story's essential elements. Once the sites are finished, students will explore the other teams' sites and rate them according to a rubric designed by the class.

Materials You Need

- *Webmasters* reproducible (page 85)
- One or more stories to use for the activity
- Access to Internet-connected computers
- Web design software or basic HTML tutorial
- LCD multimedia projector and computer
- Overhead projector and supplies

Getting Ready

Decide up front if all teams will use the same story or each choose their own as the basis for their Web sites. Make story selections accordingly. Choose another story that is familiar to students to use during the modeling segment of the activity. Create a list of sample Web sites to use for modeling and discussion. You may also want to create your own Web site based on the model story. Make student handouts using the *Webmasters* reproducible.

Students may need a short tutorial on Web design or basic HTML before beginning the activity. They may also need time outside of class to work on their Web sites, so consider extending the activity over a period of time in order to accommodate the students' needs.

Introducing the Activity

Ask students to explain the purposes of a Web site—who or what might have one, and how are the sites designed? Ask for examples of sites that students visit frequently.

Explain that in this activity, students will become Webmasters, designing their own Web sites to demonstrate their understanding of stories they have read. After the sites are completed, students will rate the sites using a rubric developed by the class and give awards to the sites that best represent the stories and their essential elements.

Modeling the Activity

1. Using an LCD multimedia projector, show students some sample Web sites. Talk about the features of a well-designed site. Have students take notes during this step, or record their ideas on the board or an overhead transparency. Some guiding criteria might include:

   - **Content**—What is the Web site's purpose? Is it obvious or confusing?
   - **Navigation**—How easy is it to find what you are looking for on the site?
   - **Uniformity**—Are content and design elements consistent?
   - **Graphics**—Do the images enhance or detract from the site's purpose?
   - **Appearance**—Is the site easy to load and does it look good on the screen?
   - **Completeness**—Does the site provide all of the information you want on the topic?

2. Introduce your model story. Ask students to summarize the story orally, recalling important details and retelling important events. Using an overhead transparency, take notes, reinforcing any important features, such as the basic plot, sequencing, main idea, characters, conflict, and resolution.

3. Brainstorm with students how they could use a Web site to convey the story's main features and supporting elements. Sketch out what the site might look like on the board or on a transparency. If possible, show students a sample Web site you created based on the story and have them compare their ideas with your own design.

4. Next, work with students to create a rubric that will be used to evaluate each Web site. Incorporate the ideas generated in Steps 1 and 2 above, adding other details as needed. Create a formalized, word-processed draft of the rubric. Then, have students give additional input before revising and making a final version of the rubric. Make copies of the rubric for students.

Activity in Practice

1. Have students work in small teams. Distribute copies of the *Webmasters* handout to them.

2. Instruct students to complete Part 1 of the handout using the rubric developed in class and complete Parts 2 and 3 of the handout before starting to work on their designs at the computer.

3. Once all of the students or teams have finished their Web sites, ask them to check their own sites against the rubric and revise them as needed.

4. Host a Web site fair for students to explore each other's Web sites and have them rate the sites based on the rubric. Present awards to the top three Webmasters based on their scores.

Extensions

This activity could be revised to be an ongoing project, where students create one main Web site with subsequent Web pages for different stories or texts they read. Students could also create Web quests based on ideas from the texts, exploring other content areas associated with the original text's content or story line.

Literary Logos

Description

In order to do well on standardized tests, students must be able to analyze relationships between the overarching message of a reading passage and the details. In this activity, students will act as clothing designers to create T-shirts that reveal a text's main idea along with its supporting details. The front of each T-shirt will sport a logo, slogan, phrase, or image that embodies the text's main idea. Supporting details will appear on the back of the shirt to explain or support the T-shirt's design. These details might be presented in the form of a top-ten list, random key words, quotations, phrases, or other small images or pictures.

Skills/State Standards
X Identifying main idea and supporting details

Materials You Need

- *Literary Logos* reproducible (page 86)
- Sample T-shirt designs (actual or digital) with images on both front and back
- Stories or texts for the modeling segment and activity itself
- Art supplies for creating T-shirts (construction paper, markers, glue, scissors, etc.)
- Overhead projector and supplies
- LCD multimedia projector and computer (optional)

Getting Ready

The day before doing this activity, ask students to wear their favorite, school-appropriate T-shirts to class. You may also want to have sample T-shirts on hand for the modeling segment of the activity. If the use of real T-shirts is not practical, consider collecting JPEG or GIF images of shirts from the Internet to serve as models.

Make student handouts using the *Literary Logos* reproducible. Make an additional copy on a transparency to use during the modeling segment.

Introducing the Activity

Ask students to share some favorite T-shirts they have owned or seen. Talk about how a T-shirt is designed, including what normally goes on the front and what goes on the back. Discuss different reasons people design T-shirts with slogans—to advertise something, to promote an idea, to express an opinion, and so on.

Explain that a T-shirt designer usually tries to get his message, purpose, or idea across by using the "less is more" concept. Discuss how T-shirts can say a lot in a small amount of space and how they make an impact on the viewer by using bold colors or lettering, simple graphics, and key words or well-chosen phrases.

Tell students that in this activity, they will design T-shirts based on a story or other text they have read. They will determine the main idea of the text and use that to develop logos, slogans, phrases, or images for the fronts of their T-shirts. Then, they will identify the text's supporting details and tailor those to fit on the backs of the T-shirts.

Modeling the Activity

1. Show students examples of T-shirts that have logos on one side and supporting images, words, or details on the other side. A concert T-shirt is a good example: the band and album name usually appear on the front with tour dates and cities on the back. Discuss how a T-shirt's main idea is expressed through the use of graphics, words, and colors.

2. Consider the differences between a logo and a slogan. Explain that a logo is an image used by a business or company to identify itself and distinguish its products from others. A logo can be a name or phrase presented in a consistent fashion or an icon of some kind. A slogan is a brief, attention-getting phrase used in advertising or a promotion.

3. Place your *Literary Logos* transparency on the overhead projector and fill it out using a story or other text familiar to students. Explain how you thought about and determined a logo or slogan to represent the main idea on the front of the T-shirt and then looked at the supporting details to come up with ideas for the back.

4. If more modeling is needed, have students help you complete another transparency using the main idea and details from another story they have read.

Activity in Practice

1. Decide beforehand if each team will read a different text or if the whole class will use the same text. This activity can also follow the reading of a text as a class.

2. Divide the class into small teams and distribute copies of the *Literary Logos* handout. Explain that although they are working in teams, every student should complete a separate handout. Later, all of the students on each team will share their ideas to develop their final T-shirt design.

3. After each team member has completed the handout, have teams discuss their ideas and come up with designs for their T-shirts.

4. Have teams share their final designs with the rest of the class, explaining the rationale behind each design.

5. Ask students how this activity helped them determine the main idea and supporting details of a text.

Extension

For an added multimedia dimension, consider allowing students to create electronic images of their T-shirt designs using a drawing or graphic design software program.

Perfect Pitch

Description

In this activity, students will get hands-on practice summarizing a longer text in an abbreviated and entertaining version for an audience. Assuming the role of scriptwriters, students will take the essential details and features of a narrative and condense it into a short, two-minute or less "teaser pitch." Each team will use their teaser pitch to try to sell the story as a movie concept to an audience of film producers (their student peers). Those pitches that make the cut will advance to the next round, where a longer "story pitch" will be presented. Finally, the top pitches will be "optioned" (purchased for consideration) by the audience and receive prizes for fluid and concise storytelling, originality, and entertainment value.

Skills/State Standards

X Summarizing and paraphrasing

X Story structure and elements

X Identifying cause and effect

X Understanding sequence and chronology

This activity requires students to focus on the major themes and elements of a story. The teaser pitch encourages students to introduce the genre, scope, and main idea of the text. In the story pitch, students will focus on details about characters, setting, conflict, climax, and resolution. As students present and listen to the pitches, they are also developing oral presentation and listening skills in an engaging and challenging way.

Materials You Need

- *Perfect Pitch* reproducible (page 87)
- Stories for the modeling segment and activity itself
- Stopwatch or timer
- Overhead projector and supplies

Getting Ready

Prepare a few sample teaser and story pitches based on familiar stories, books, or movies. Write these examples on transparencies and share them with students as you model the activity. To ensure a variety of pitches, generate a list of stories for students to choose from or approve appropriate independent reading material in advance.

Make student handouts using the *Perfect Pitch* reproducible.

Introducing the Activity

Name a recent or popular film, and ask students to think about its plot and major features. Then, ask them to summarize the film in just three sentences. What details would they include and why? What if they had to condense a whole book or long story in three sentences—would it be easier or more challenging?

Tell students that reducing an entire story to a few words is both a skill and an art—and something they are fully capable of doing. Remind students that summarizing is an essential skill that they will need to know for standardized tests. This activity provides hands-on practice with summarizing in a fun and offbeat context.

Explain that in this activity, students will pretend to be scriptwriters, pitching their ideas for "movies" (the stories or books they have read) to "film producers" (their classmates). Their scripts will come from recently read texts (stories, independent reading, or assigned stories for the activity). Working in teams of two, students will draft teaser pitches and longer story pitches. In Round One, each pair will pitch their teaser to an audience of peers. The best teasers will move on Round Two, where the longer story pitches will be presented. The best pitches will win by being "optioned" or chosen for purchase by the film-producer audience.

Modeling the Activity

1. Explain the two types of pitches that students will be creating in this activity, beginning with the teaser pitch: The *teaser pitch* is essentially a skeleton of a story pitch, usually done in three sentences. It covers the basis, genre, and scope of the film. The first sentence normally introduces the characters, the second illustrates their conflict, and the third hooks the audience and makes them want to hear more. A teaser is usually one to two minutes in length.

2. Using your overhead transparencies, share some teaser pitches based on familiar stories or popular films. Here is an example of a teaser pitch for Shakespeare's *Romeo and Juliet*:

   Verona, Italy, circa 1300. Two teenagers from warring families do the impossible—they fall in love. Their love seems stronger than blood but proves just as deadly as hate.

3. Next, explain the story pitch: The *story pitch* is a longer, more detailed version of the story. It starts with a logline, or hook sentence, and then covers the rest of the story's key events and special qualities. A good story pitch includes elements common in most stories, like a hero, conflict, climax, and conclusion. Yet, it also highlights what makes the story unique. For this activity, the story pitch should be about five minutes in length.

4. Show students your transparency of sample story pitches. Read each one aloud with energy and excitement. Ask students to comment on your reading, noting what made the story come alive during each pitch.

5. Offer students a few pointers to keep their pitches from becoming too boring or routine:

   - Don't compare your story to others too much, such as "It's *Goldilocks* meets the *Three Little Pigs*."
   - Remember, you are telling a story, not simply listing events in order.
   - Do not include too many subplots or extra details. Keep the story streamlined and focused on two or three characters to make it easier to follow.
   - Describe the characters vividly so that your listeners will picture who might play the part, but do not offer names of specific actors.

6. If time permits, develop a basic rubric with students that includes the necessary oral presentation skills as well as features to include in the teaser and story pitches.

Activity in Practice

1. Divide the class into teams of two. Ask each pair of students to select a story as the basis for their teaser and story pitches. Alternatively, assign each pair a different story or text.
2. Distribute copies of the *Perfect Pitch* handout for students to complete with their partners.
3. Give students time to practice their teaser and story pitches, timing each other to make sure they stay within the time limits. Have copies of the rubric available or have students use their completed handouts as checklists to make sure they have included all of the required elements in their pitches.
4. When students are ready for Round One, select one student from each pair to present the teaser. As the rest of the class listens, have students rank each teaser pitch according to the rubric or other grading scale to keep track of the teasers that stand out from the rest.
5. In Round Two, the partner who did not present the teaser pitch will give the story pitch, if that pair was selected to move on.
6. Once Round Two is over, have the class (i.e., the "film producers") select the top pitches to receive "option awards."

Extensions

As an alternative to this activity, consider having students write haikus based on entire story plots. With only 17 syllables and three lines available to them, students will have to maximize each word to get the most important features across.

As a springboard to a creative writing assignment, have students draft teasers for story ideas and pitch them to each other in small teams. Then, have students give each other feedback before drafting their longer versions.

Laundry Line

Description

Interpreting and analyzing the motivations, thoughts, and attitudes of a character is a common standard addressed on state tests. This activity highlights these aspects of character analysis.

Skills/State Standards

X Analyzing character

In this activity, traits of several characters will be represented on pieces of paper clothing hung on clotheslines in the classroom. Students will be divided into teams with each team assigned a different character. Given a time limit, students will then work with their teams to sort the laundry by deciding which clothing items belong to their team's character. Some details could be representative of several characters, so students will have to draw upon their interpretive and analytical skills when selecting the clothing. Once they have sorted the laundry, they must put together the wardrobe of that character and explain how all of the pieces fit together, both literally and metaphorically.

Materials You Need

- *Laundry Line* reproducible (page 88)
- Stories (with characters) for the activity
- Clotheslines and clothespins
- Small laundry-style baskets or boxes (one for each team)
- Colored construction paper and scissors
- Poster board and glue or tape
- Stopwatch or timer
- Overhead projector and supplies

Getting Ready

This activity will be more successful with a large number of characters, as well as a large selection of clothing and accessory items for each character. The clothing and accessories could represent actual items described in the story, or they could be more symbolic in nature. For example, a backpack could represent a character who dreams of travel but never takes a trip away from home.

One way to prepare for this activity is to make all of the paper clothing pieces yourself. Alternatively, you could have students make the clothing items over the course of several weeks, saving the activity itself until the end of a unit. After each story in a particular reading unit, have students make appropriate clothing and accessory items out of construction paper until it is time to play the game. Then, add more of your own created items to challenge the students and increase the number of items they must sort. Use the patterns on the *Laundry Line* reproducible, adding other pieces as needed.

Introducing the Activity

Read the following description and ask students to picture the person in their minds:

> Six-foot-tall male
> Old, worn leather jacket with silver studs on the collar
> Long, shaggy, dark brown hair
> Torn, faded jeans
> Canvas, high-top sneakers with holes in the bottoms
> Black T-shirt with sleeves torn off

Next, ask students to describe the person. What do they think he likes to do? What are his friends like? What kind of music does he listen to? What is his favorite subject in school? How old is he? What is his name?

After hearing a variety of responses and ideas, explain to students that the reader often has to interpret clues in order to figure out a character's motivations, thoughts, and attitudes. Sometimes these clues are obvious, but sometimes they are very subtle, such as how the character walks in her shoes or what colors she likes to wear. Looks can also be misleading, and there can be hidden feelings or hopes beneath the surface appearance of a character.

Tell students that in this activity, they will work in teams to interpret and analyze a character from a story they have read. To do this, they will try to collect the laundry of their assigned character from a series of clotheslines hung in the classroom. Once the time is up and they have gathered all of the pieces they think they need, students will sort them by creating a wardrobe for that character, including accessories and other items they have chosen. Finally, they will explain to the class how the items go together and represent or reveal something about the character and his influence on the story.

Modeling the Activity

1. Select a character that is familiar to students and have them brainstorm a list of her qualities and attributes. List these traits on a transparency. Then, ask students to recall any significant clothing or personal items that the character may have possessed in the story. List those on the transparency as well.

2. Ask students to consider how each article of clothing or personal item represents something about the character. Discuss what items might be used to represent the other qualities and attributes on the list.

3. Explore how the character influenced the story and its elements, including the setting, plot, conflict, and resolution. How might those influences be represented through personal or clothing items that belong to the character?

4. Tell students that when selecting items from the clotheslines, they must think about both the literal and figurative aspects of their assigned characters, since a variety of items will be hung on the lines from which they may choose. Explain that in some cases an item may be appropriate for more than one character.

Activity in Practice

1. Divide the class into small teams. Give each team a laundry basket or box and a character's name.

2. Explain the basic rules of the game: Given a time limit, each team must work together to gather their character's laundry by selecting items carefully. If students think they have chosen an item incorrectly, they can hang it back on the line or trade it for another item with another team.

3. Start the timer and have teams begin collecting their characters' laundry.

4. When the time is up, have each team sort the laundry they have collected and shape it into a wardrobe. Remind each team that they must be prepared to explain why each item belongs in the character's wardrobe and how it contributes to the character's influence on the story as a whole.

5. Have teams present their characters' wardrobes to the class in a character fashion show by gluing or taping the items to poster board and explaining their choices.

Extensions

For written practice, consider having each team member write down an explanation of each piece of the character's wardrobe to be used as the basis for a character analysis essay.

Have a Characters Come to Life Day. Allow students to dress up in clothing and accessories that are representative of characters from stories recently read as a class.

Textual Duo

Description

This activity uses the format of a memory matching game to encourage students to make connections within a text and between texts.

In the game Duo, cards are placed facedown on a surface. The face sides of the cards contain elements from a story—setting, characters, problem, resolution, events, etc. Students are paired off and each takes a turn by flipping over two cards. The object of the game is to make a match by explaining how the two cards are similar to or different from one another. If a player thinks she has a match, she explains why and keeps the cards. If not, she turns the cards facedown again, and the other player takes a turn by flipping over two cards to make a match. Each player can challenge the other player's explanations. The player with the most matches at the end of the game wins.

The game cards can contain details from one specific text, two or more texts, different types of texts (expository, narrative, etc.), or texts with different purposes—whatever best reflects the skills you want students to target. The content of the cards can vary as well, focusing on similar or contrasting elements from two or more texts or highlighting features from one specific text.

Materials You Need

- Stories or texts to use for the activity
- Index cards or blank playing cards (one set for each pair of players)
- Overhead projector and supplies

Getting Ready

Each pair of players will need a set of game cards. The sets can be similar to or different from one another to encourage variety. The sets may also contain an odd number of cards, not completely "matching," to add an extra challenge as students try to make connections between cards that initially seem contrasting or dissimilar.

Making sets of playing cards may take some time. To include students in the process, you might want to distribute index cards to them and have them select elements, details, and excerpts from the texts to use for the content of the cards.

Introducing the Activity

Ask students if they have ever played some kind of matching game. Ask them what the purpose of a matching game is. After discussing their responses, explain that pairing two things together as a match is based on comparing and contrasting them to one another. When trying to match two things, the object is to find what is similar between them, or in some cases, exactly alike. Remind students that two contrasting or slightly different things can also make a pair—a left and right shoe, a red light and a green light, or the sun and the moon—depending on the context and each item's own qualities.

Tell students that in this activity, they will compare and contrast elements within one or more texts. They will play against a partner to match up cards to make a pair. To make a matching pair, they must explain the connections, similarities, or differences between the information presented on the face of the cards.

Modeling the Activity

1. Make an overhead transparency of some sample Duo cards based on a familiar story. Ask students to help you match the cards to form pairs. Solicit input from them as to how each pair matches up—what is similar or different about the cards that, when they are put together, forms a match of some kind?

2. Tell students that when playing this game, they must explain each match in order to keep the two cards. In some cases, they may not find a match and will have to place the cards facedown again, trying to remember what was on the face of each card for a future turn.

3. The opposing player can challenge a match if he doesn't think the explanation makes clear the comparison or contrast. If the explanation does not make sense, the opposing player says "Duo-ver" and then takes a turn. If the explanation does make sense, the opposing player says "Duo," and the first player gets another turn. If the players cannot reach an agreement, a referee (the teacher) can be called in to decide if the pair of cards is a match or not. The player who makes the most matches wins the game.

Activity in Practice

1. Divide the class into teams of two students and give each pair a set of game cards.
2. Have students shuffle the cards and place them facedown on a playing surface.
3. Review the rules of the game and tell students to keep track of their cards.
4. Once all of the cards are gone, or matched, have students tally up their pairs and declare a winner for each game.
5. Ask students to share their most interesting or clever matches with the rest of the class.
6. Discuss with students how playing this game might be helpful when trying to make comparisons or recognize contrasts on the reading portions of the standardized tests they will take.

Extension

This activity could be altered to address cause and effect in a text. To make a match, students would have to pair each cause with its effect and explain the relationship.

One Thing Leads to Another

Description

This activity will bring cause-and-effect relationships to life, using students as the primary vehicles. After reading a text, students will be divided into small teams and each student will be given one or more events to personify. Each team will work together to decide how the events fit into a cause-and-effect pattern and create a graphic organizer to show those relationships. Then, each team will devise a unique way to show the class how these relationships fit together to create a whole. Team presentations may involve performing a skit, unveiling a spectacular visual, singing a song, or some other representation that is out of the ordinary.

Skills/State Standards

X Identifying cause and effect

X Understanding sequence and chronology

X Using graphic organizers

Materials You Need

- Stories for the modeling segment and activity itself
- Index cards
- Poster board or drawing paper
- Overhead projector and supplies

Getting Ready

This activity can be done using a different story for each group or one story for the whole class. Once you have decided which stories to use, create a list of events from each one. Write each event on a separate index card, making sure to include at least one event per student in class. Then select another story to use for modeling the activity. Prepare a sample presentation to demonstrate to the class.

Reviewing different types of graphic organizers beforehand will spark students' imaginations for formats they can use during the activity.

Introducing the Activity

Read aloud the following statements to your class:

- The pepperoni pizza with extra onions and garlic arrives.
- Joe's stomach starts grumbling.
- Joe calls Ziggy's Pizza Parlor.
- Joe watches a commercial advertising fast food.
- Joe has a serious case of indigestion.

Ask students to tell you the most logical order for those statements. After they make some suggestions, ask them why they think the events would occur in that order—how are the events related? Lead students to see that cause and effect played a role in the sequencing of the events. Tell them that cause-and-effect relationships play a big part in events all around them, as well as in the stories and texts they read. Causes can spur on events and create effects, which in turn can become new causes for other events, and so on. Recognizing cause-and-effect relationships can be key to understanding a text. It is also an important skill on which students will be tested.

Tell students that in this activity, they will become the causes and effects in a story. Working in teams, they will fit the events together into a coherent pattern and represent that pattern visually by creating a graphic organizer. Finally, they will demonstrate the pattern in some kind of unique presentation, such as a skit, song, or news report.

Modeling the Activity

1. Using an overhead transparency, brainstorm with students some major events from a story they know well. Have them help you sequence these events in terms of their cause-and-effect relationships.

2. Ask students how these relationships could be shown on paper via a graphic organizer of some kind. If they want to use a familiar format, try that first, and then lead them to step outside the box in terms of playing with the format.

3. Using the organizer you have developed, brainstorm potential presentation formats, keeping in mind the types of causes and effects involved in the story.

4. Show students your own short presentation for the model story to provide them with additional ideas.

Activity in Practice

1. Divide the class into small teams and give each team member at least one event card. Make sure that each team has a full set of events in order to complete a cause-and-effect sequence based on the text.

2. After students have figured out how to sequence their events into a cause-and-effect pattern, give each team a sheet of poster board or drawing paper on which to create their graphic organizer.

3. As teams begin brainstorming presentation ideas, circle around the room, offering suggestions and encouraging creativity.

4. Have each team share their graphic organizer before giving their presentation.

Extension

To give students more individual practice, try a variation of this activity based on the game of solitaire. In this version, story elements, events, and other details are divided and shuffled in a pack of story playing cards. Students must follow the rules of solitaire to create "suits" or chains of causes and effects, until all of the chains fit together into one cohesive whole.

5

Third Eye

Description

In this activity, students will use visualization skills in tandem with personal experience to make predictions about a text before they read it.

Each team of students will be given a collage of pictures in the shape of an eye. The picture in the pupil, or center of the eye, will show the main idea of the story. The pictures in the surrounding parts of the eye, or the iris and white, will present supporting details, such as key events, characters, problems, and resolutions. Students will study the eye and use the pictures to make predictions about the text they will read. Then, after reading the text, they will compare their predictions to the actual text.

> **Skills/State Standards**
> X Making predictions
> X Identifying main idea and supporting details

Materials You Need

- *Third Eye* reproducible (page 89)
- Stories for the modeling segment and activity itself
- Poster board or transparencies
- Overhead projector and supplies or computer and LCD multimedia projector

Getting Ready

Select two stories to use with this activity—one for the modeling segment and one for the activity itself. The first should be a story familiar to all of the students, while the second should be a story they have never read. Provide copies of the second story for students to read after they have made their predictions.

Once you have chosen the stories, you will need to prepare a third-eye collage for each. Enlarge the image of the eye on page 89 to use as a pattern or simply create your own. Make sure that the image in the pupil of each eye represents the main idea and that the images in the rest of the eye represent supporting details. Be sure to select pictures that are not too literal, which will allow room for interpretation and a wider variety of predictions from students. Make photocopies of the finished collages for students or, if possible, create electronic versions or color transparencies of the eyes.

Make student handouts using the *Third Eye* reproducible.

Introducing the Activity

Choose a book with which students are not familiar. The cover should be very graphic or visual and leave room for interpretation. Cover or remove the title of the book and then show the book to students. Ask students to make a prediction about the content or storyline of the book. After discussing some possibilities, ask them what it was about the cover illustration or graphics that clued them in to the main idea of the story.

Tell students that making predictions is something they do every day, using clues and their own experiences and knowledge. Sometimes the clues are very obvious, and other times they are quite subtle. Tell students that in this activity, they will practice using their skills of visual interpretation to make predictions about a text they are going to read.

Modeling the Activity

1. Show students your sample third-eye collage based on a story they have read, but do not tell them the title of the story.
2. Ask students to look at the pupil of the eye and tell you what the story's main idea might be, based on that picture.
3. Then, direct students to look at the other pictures for additional clues about the story.
4. After they have made connections between all of the pictures, invite students to guess what story the pictures represent.
5. Explain that in this activity, they will use images to make predictions about a story they will read, determining its main idea and supporting details.

Activity in Practice

1. Divide the class into small teams.
2. Distribute copies of the third-eye collage you have created that is based on an unfamiliar story along with copies of the *Third Eye* handout. Have students complete the handout as they decode the images on the collage to make predictions.
3. After all of the teams have finished, ask them to share their predictions.
4. Pass out copies of the story and give students time to read it. Then, discuss and compare the students' predictions with the actual story.

Extension

Have each team read a different story and create its own third-eye collage to exchange with another team.

Cliff-Hanger

Description

This activity is designed to engage students' prediction skills while they are actually reading a text. Students will read a narrative selection aloud as a class, pausing at marked prediction points in the text. At these points, students will work with partners to compose entertaining "cliff-hangers" reminiscent of old-fashioned movie or television show trailers that leave the audience hanging as to what will happen next. Then students will make a prediction about how the cliff-hanger is resolved. Each pair of students will read their cliff-hanger and prediction aloud. The class will then vote for the most entertaining version, as well as the one that sounds the most likely to happen. After all of the cliff-hangers have been read, the class will continue to read aloud, pausing again at the next prediction point. At the end of the story, students will add up the votes to see which team was deemed the most creative and which was the most on target with their predictions.

> ### Skills/State Standards
> ✗ Making predictions
> ✗ Identifying cause and effect

Materials You Need

- Narrative texts for the modeling segment and activity itself
- Overhead projector and supplies

Getting Ready

You will need to select at least two narrative texts that are unfamiliar to students—a short one to use for modeling the activity and a longer one for the activity itself. Divide each narrative into sections, breaking it up at natural prediction points. This will make it easier for students to create cliff-hangers, as well as keep them from reading ahead. Copy the shorter narrative onto a transparency to use during the modeling segment. Prepare a few fun cliff-hangers based on the short text you selected. You will share these examples with students when you model the activity. Provide copies of the longer narrative on paper, using a separate sheet for each section. Make one copy of the longer narrative for each pair of students.

Introducing the Activity

Read the following passage to students:

> The diver stood on the highest platform, poised above the water. He stared down at the smooth, cool surface and closed his eyes, clasping his hands above his head.

Ask students to guess what might happen next, but not to say anything out loud. Then, read them this example of a cliff-hanger and a prediction:

> Will the diver take the plunge or will he chicken out?
> Tune in next time to see Keith make the perfect dive and help his team go on
> to win the district title!

Did students think the diver would actually make the dive? What clues did they use to make their predictions?

Tell students that making predictions is something that all good readers do. It helps keep them interested in the text and, therefore, they get more out of reading. Explain that in this activity, students will make predictions of their own. Reading a narrative aloud together as a class, they will pause at the end of each section and work with partners to write cliff-hangers and then predict what will happen next. Students will vote for the most plausible, as well as the most entertaining, cliff-hangers. At the end of the story, they will tally the votes to see which teams were the most creative and which ones were the most accurate.

Modeling the Activity

1. Using an overhead projector, show students the first paragraph or segment of a short story they have not read. After reading the text together, ask them to make a silent prediction as to what might happen next.
2. Ask for volunteers to share their predictions, and select one or more from which to craft a cliff-hanger together. Share your own cliff-hangers for the same text excerpt.
3. Discuss with students any tips they should follow when crafting their cliff-hangers—using questions, adding interesting details, choosing dramatic words, etc.

Activity in Practice

1. Divide the class into pairs and distribute copies of the first story segment.
2. Select a volunteer to read aloud, or read the first segment to the class yourself.
3. Pause at the end of the segment and ask students to work quietly with their partners to brainstorm and draft their cliff-hangers and predictions.
4. Have each pair take turns reading their cliff-hangers and predictions aloud. Keep track of the votes each pair receives on the board or on an overhead transparency.
5. Continue in the same manner for the rest of the story. At the end, tally the votes and declare winners for the most creative cliff-hangers and most accurate predictions.

Extensions

This activity could also be done in the style of a silent auction, where each student writes down a prediction at each prediction point and turns in the paper to you. Then, after the entire story is finished, each correct prediction receives a point.

The Great Debate

Description

Many students have difficulty recognizing when they are making inferences, or realizing that they can use their own wealth of knowledge in combination with textual clues to piece together a bigger picture about a theme, issue, or concept.

```
╔══════════════════════════════════╗
║  Skills/State Standards          ║
║  X  Making inferences and drawing║
║     conclusions                  ║
╚══════════════════════════════════╝
```

In this activity, students will actively gain experience recognizing and using inferences to help draw conclusions and make generalizations about what they read under the guise of defending their own ideas and points of view. The class will be divided into two teams and an audience, with students switching roles for each debate. Each team will be presented with a different side of a story to defend with evidence from the text. Each side includes potential inferences, conclusions, or generalizations about the text that the reader could make, depending on her own experiences, knowledge, and clues from the text itself. Teams will be given a set amount of time to argue their positions, either defending or negating them with textual evidence and life experiences, then drawing conclusions or making generalizations, if relevant. The student audience will decide which team wins each debate.

Materials You Need

- *The Great Debate* reproducible (page 90)
- Texts for the modeling segment and activity itself
- Index cards with "sides" from selected text
- Timer or stopwatch
- Overhead projector and supplies

Getting Ready

Students should be made familiar with the differences between an inference, a conclusion, and a generalization. Make a transparency using *The Great Debate* reproducible to illustrate these differences. When selecting a text for the activity, choose one that is rich with implications from which students can make inferences. (Students should also have previously read the text but not discussed it in class or in groups.) Include possible inferences that could be argued as valid or not, so that each team has an opportunity to defend its position. Conclusions and generalizations could also be used, depending on the text.

It will also be helpful to the teams if each student has a copy of the text to use when arguing a point, especially if the sides used on the cards include excerpts from the text. Another timesaver would be to give each team a copy of all the possible cards before the debate begins, so that each team can prepare both sides of the argument. Then, when the debate begins, the moderator can draw a card randomly from the pile for each set of teams debating.

The types of inferences presented on the cards for the debate should vary. One variation could include a quotation from the text and then a statement or question, such as:

> "The wolf licked his lips and smiled as he eyed Little Red Riding Hood as she skipped through the forest."
>
> Potential Inference: The wolf is hungry and wants to eat Little Red.

If appropriate, two potential inferences could be offered, with each team defending one of the two choices. Another possibility is for one team to express an inference based on an excerpt or description from the text, and for the opposing team to refute it.

Another format for card content could include accurate inferences, followed by a potential conclusion or generalization that could be made based on that inference:

> Inference from paragraph 5: The wolf is going to outsmart Little Red Riding Hood.
>
> Potential Generalization: All wolves are sneaky tricksters.

Introducing the Activity

Ask students to define the word *debate*. If any students have formal experience with debating, invite them to share their knowledge about what it means to defend a position with evidence. If necessary, brainstorm with students about what makes a good argument—what does someone need to do in order to make his view seem convincing and plausible to someone else?

Tell students that in this activity, they will get the chance to take sides and defend their positions with evidence. Explain that the sides they will argue will actually be potential inferences, conclusions, or even generalizations a reader might make about a text while reading it. It will be each team's job to argue one side or the other by using the text as support, along with their own experiences and knowledge. Then, the audience will decide which team has won the argument based on the evidence provided.

Modeling the Activity

1. Use the overhead transparency of *The Great Debate* reproducible to review with students the difference between an inference, a conclusion, and a generalization. Use examples from a familiar story to illustrate the differences among the three.
2. Select one of the three examples discussed previously and role-play how you would argue

both sides using evidence from the text and your own experiences. Have the students give feedback as to how well your arguments were supported and explained. Present at least one faulty argument so that students can critique it and use it to guide their own debating techniques.

3. Develop a checklist with students that explains what a debater should include in a successful argument:

   • Sufficient evidence: Specific examples from the text (excerpts, main idea, summarization, quotations, etc.)
   • Experiences and knowledge that can support an inference
   • The use of inductive or deductive reasoning, if applicable

   Inductive reasoning is the process of offering a suitable number of specific examples to prove a generalization—from the specific to the general.

   Deductive reasoning moves from the general to the specific, following the syllogism of the following: If A = B (all cats have claws) and C = A (Spike is a cat), then C = B (Spike has claws).

4. Together, create a rubric based on the checklist for the audience to use to rate each debater for each round. For sample criteria, ask the school's speech/debate coach or download an example from the Internet.

Activity in Practice

1. Divide the class into four or more teams, so that at least two teams will debate while the other teams form the audience. The size of the teams will depend on how many students and debate cards there are. Every student on every team should get at least one chance to debate and/or to prepare the argument for a card.

2. Assign a timekeeper from the audience for each card round. You may want to decide upon other rules with the class beforehand. Brief all students on how each round will be judged by the audience, according to the rubric developed in the modeling segment.

3. After all the teams have had a chance to debate several cards, tally up the points from the rating sheets and declare a team winner.

4. Conclude by having each winning team prepare an explanation on how this activity helped improve their inference-making skills and present it to the class.

Extensions

To provide additional practice with expressing inferences, conclusions, and generalizations, have your class play this cumulative game. Working in small teams, the first student makes an inference, the next makes another inference, the third draws a conclusion, and the fourth makes a generalization. Students may use the handout for reference and/or simple texts or pictures that have been provided.

Got Your Back

Description

This activity will require active participation by all students as they each try to determine a different word's meaning based on its context. The students will become walking billboards. On the fronts of their shirts, they will each wear a card on which a word with an unknown meaning (a different word for each student) is written; on the backs of their shirts, they will each wear a card containing the word's dictionary definitions. Students will then walk around the classroom, as other students read the definitions silently and create sentences using the words. The students formulating sentences will try to be creative without revealing too much of the words' meanings. Each student will keep a running list of the sentences created by his peers. The object of the game is for each student to figure out the meaning of his word exclusively through the context clues given by the other students.

Skills/State Standards

X Using context clues

Materials You Need

- *Got Your Back* reproducible (page 91)
- Index cards
- Adhesive tape or large safety pins
- Overhead projector and supplies

Getting Ready

Prepare two transparencies to use during the modeling segment of the activity. The first should include the four main types of context clues:

- **Definition/Explanation Clues**—when an unfamiliar word's meaning is explained within the same sentence as the word itself is used

- **Restatement/Synonym Clues**—when a word is restated in a simpler form or clarified with a synonym or similar phrase

- **Contrast/Antonym Clues**—when a word's meaning is made clear through the inclusion of its opposite meaning, which is often indicated by a signal word, such as *but*, *not*, or *or*

- **Inference/General Context Clues**—when a word's meaning is revealed through other clues or content within the sentence or paragraph (The reader must make inferences about the word based on clues that appear before, within, and after a sentence containing the unfamiliar word.)

Provide an example for each type of clue. Write each example on the transparency next to or below the corresponding definition.

The second transparency should include at least two unfamiliar words and their definitions. Design the transparency so the unfamiliar words can be shown in isolation before the definitions are revealed. Choose one of the words and define it using all four types of context clues.

Next, select words to use for the activity. You will need one word per student—more if you intend to play two or more rounds of the game. The words can come from vocabulary lists, texts students will be reading, or words they may encounter on standardized tests. Write each word on a separate index card. Write the word and its definition on a second card.

Finally, make student handouts using the *Got Your Back* reproducible.

Introducing the Activity

Read aloud a sentence that contains an unfamiliar word and ask students to tell you what the word means. As they make guesses about the word's meaning, ask students for evidence to support their guesses. Tell them that their evidence should be based upon the context clues within the sentence itself. Explain that using context clues to decipher meanings of unfamiliar words is a valuable skill to have—one that can build their vocabularies and help them figure out word meanings on standardized tests.

Tell students that in this activity, they will use context clues provided by classmates to determine the meanings of words they will be assigned. Explain that on the fronts of their shirts, they will wear cards containing unknown words; on the backs, they will wear cards with the words' definitions. Since they will not be able see the definitions, they will need to walk around the classroom, collecting sentences created by their classmates which will help reveal the meanings of the mysterious words through context clues. Students will then use those sentences as tools to decode the words' meanings and write their own definitions.

Modeling the Activity

1. Using the transparency you prepared, review with students the four main types of context clues: definition/explanation, restatement/synonym, contrast/antonym, and inference/ general context.

2. Show students an unfamiliar word. Ask them to guess the word's meaning and generate a few possible definitions.

3. Reveal the word's definition. Encourage students to help you generate sentences containing each type of context clue, and write them on the transparency.

4. Show students another unfamiliar word. This time, ask them to think about the word's meaning silently, without revealing what they think it might mean.

5. Next, display the four different context-clue sentences you have written (one for each major type of context clue) that help define the word.

6. Ask students to identify the type of context clue used in each sentence. Then, ask them to offer a definition of the word, based on the clues in the sentences.

Activity in Practice

1. Distribute copies of the *Got Your Back* handout to students.

2. Label each student, front and back, with two index cards—one containing a word and the other containing the same word and its definition. Use tape or safety pins to attach the cards to students' shirts. Take care that students don't see their own words' definitions.

3. Decide if the activity will be timed or played like a race to the finish. Then, tell students to circulate around the room, gathering as many context clues as possible from classmates and recording those clues on their handouts. Encourage students to follow these guidelines:

   • Try to get classmates to offer sentences that are rich in context clues.
     A variety of types of clues will make it easier to guess the meanings of the words.

   • Don't be too literal when creating context clues for classmates.
     Using the clues to decode the words' meanings should still be a challenge.

4. Once they have collected a set number of sentences, have students use their clues to write dictionary-style definitions of their words.

5. Have students remove the cards from each other's backs so they can compare their own definitions to the real ones.

6. Ask students to share the most unique and entertaining sentences they collected. Then, ask whose definitions came closest to the actual meanings.

Extension

Try this variation of the activity to focus on the structure of words, including prefixes, suffixes, and Greek or Latin roots. List word parts and their meanings on cards and tape them to students' backs. As students walk around, they must ask their peers for sentences containing words with the word part. As students record the sentences, they will try to figure out both the word part and what the word part means.

Fact-Checker Challenge

Description

Distinguishing between fact and opinion can be a challenge for even the most careful reader. When confronted with an expository text, students may assume that everything they read is true, forgetting that the author's opinion may actually influence their understanding. This activity targets facts

and opinions head-on by giving students the opportunity to examine them with a critical eye in a fun context. Assuming the role of fact checkers, students will preview a list of "facts" taken from three short expository texts they will later read. Before tackling the texts, they must decide whether the excerpts are truly facts or opinions disguised as facts. Then, as pairs of students read the texts together, their task will be to locate each excerpt and determine whether or not their first assumption was correct. The first pair to correctly locate and identify all of the excerpts will win the Fact-Checker Challenge.

Materials You Need

- Articles for the modeling segment and activity itself
- Variety of colored highlighters (one per student)
- Overhead projector and supplies

Getting Ready

Your selection of texts for this activity will be crucial. Be sure to choose pieces that include factual statements, as well as statements that reveal the authors' own perspectives. You will need one short text for the modeling segment and three texts for the activity itself.

Make a transparency of the modeling text, along with a short list of "facts" (some facts, some opinions) taken from the text. You can use these later to demonstrate the activity.

Provide copies of the other three texts for each pair of students. Then, make a list of "facts" (again, some facts, some opinions) taken from all three texts and type them up on one page. Create a box on the right side of the page that contains two columns—one labeled FACT and the other labeled OPINION. Make a copy of this "fact sheet" for each student pair.

Finally, prepare a transparency with brief definitions of fact and opinion:

- A *fact* is a statement that can be proven true by consulting a reliable source.
- An *opinion* is a belief based on a writer's attitude or values.

Be prepared to provide examples of each.

Introducing the Activity

Read aloud the following statement: "School is cool." Ask students whether the statement is true or not. You will probably get differing responses. Next, read this statement: "School starts at [time] each morning." Ask students to explain the difference between the two statements. Lead them to see that the first statement is an opinion—although it could be supported with evidence, it cannot be proven as an absolute truth. It is a belief based on the speaker's own point of view. The second statement, on the other hand, is a fact that can be proven by reliable sources.

Explain that fact checkers play an important role in making sure that what goes into print is correct and verifiable, especially in news stories. Fact checkers look for facts and make sure that they are corroborated by reliable sources. Opinions can sometimes be disguised as facts, however, especially when they are stated strongly. A careful reader is able to recognize the difference between fact and opinion and not get sidetracked by an author's perspective.

Tell students that in this activity, they will act as fact checkers in search of verifiable facts and misleading opinions. Working with partners, they will first review "facts" taken from texts they will read. Then, as they read the texts themselves, students will evaluate the "facts" in context, comparing them to their original assumptions. The first fact-checker pair to identify the excerpts as facts or opinions correctly wins the challenge.

Modeling the Activity

1. Using the overhead transparency, briefly review the definitions of a fact and an opinion. Provide an example or two of each.
2. Show students a list of "facts" taken from a short article or excerpt. Ask them to evaluate each "fact" as being an actual fact or an opinion in disguise.
3. Then, read the article from the transparency together, pausing as you encounter each "fact." Work with students to compare their original assumptions with the statements when read in context.

Activity in Practice

1. Divide the class into teams of two students and give each pair two highlighters of contrasting colors. Explain that they will use one color to highlight each fact and another for each opinion.
2. Distribute copies of the excerpted "facts" from the texts. Tell students to mark each excerpt as a fact or an opinion.
3. Have students read the texts again with their partners, using their highlighters to mark facts and opinions. When they are done, ask them to bring their highlighted articles and fact sheets to you for verification.

Extension

For additional practice, have students teams find facts in an article and revise them into opinions, and vice versa.

You Don't Say!

Description

To understand and answer questions about expository passages, students need to learn how to paraphrase the information accurately. This activity will give students practice paraphrasing each other's statements. At the start of the activity, one student will write a statement on a piece of paper. Then, hiding the piece of paper, she will whisper its message to the next student. The second student must listen carefully to the message, write his own paraphrase of the statement on a piece of paper, and continue the process by passing the message on to the next student. The game will continue until the message has been passed around the entire group. At that time, the class will assess whether or not the message was paraphrased accurately or, if not, which paraphrase changed its meaning.

<table>
<tr><td>Skills/State Standards

X Summarizing and paraphrasing</td></tr>
</table>

Materials You Need

- Index cards or slips of paper (one per student per round)
- Pens or pencils (one per student)

Getting Ready

Prepare a few messages of your own to use during the modeling segment of the activity. Write a good and a poor paraphrase of each message to help illustrate how paraphrasing should be done.

Whether you are using index cards or slips of paper, be sure you have enough to play several rounds of the game. Each student will need one card or slip of paper per round.

Introducing the Activity

Remind students that putting ideas into their own words first will help them better answer questions about reading-comprehension passages. Before they can rephrase an idea, students must actually process the information and make sense of it. In essence, paraphrasing a statement helps students better understand it. Offer an example of how translating a message into a new, briefer statement can make it much easier to explain and remember.

Ask students if they remember playing the game Telephone. Explain that this activity is very similar, except that students will intentionally rephrase the message each time it is passed on. Rather than repeating the message word for word, each student must paraphrase the message in her own words before passing it on to the next student.

Modeling the Activity

Share one of your sample messages with students, along with a good paraphrase of it. Explain that a good paraphrase might retain a specific detail or an important contrast from the original message. Then, provide an example of a poor paraphrase. Ask students to tell you why the second example does not work—more than likely it gets a detail wrong from the original message or fails to contrast two things properly.

Ask one volunteer to generate a message and a second volunteer to paraphrase it. Have the other students tell you if the paraphrase was accurate or not and, if not, how it could be improved.

Activity in Practice

1. Divide the class into teams of seven or more students. Have each team sit in a circle in a different part of the room.
2. Make sure every student has a pen or pencil. Give each student an index card or paper.
3. Select one student from each circle to start the game. Give those students a few minutes to create their messages and record them. Remind students to conceal their messages as they write them.
4. Once their messages are written down, instruct those students to begin the game, whispering their messages to the students sitting to their left. Those students must then silently paraphrase the messages they heard, write them down, and whisper the paraphrases to the students on their left. The game continues until the messages have made it all the way around the circles.
5. After the last student in each circle has heard the message and paraphrased it, have the class regroup. Ask the first and last student from each circle to read their messages aloud. In each case, discuss whether the paraphrase has the same meaning as the original message. If not, can students determine which paraphrases most altered the original message's meaning?

Extensions

Try repeating the activity once in larger groups and once as a whole class to see if you get more interesting results. Alternatively, you could give each group a more challenging message than one they might come up with on their own.

Examples: Carol owed Tyrone $19.95 for a book, but Tyrone owed Carol $12 for dinner.

If all of the students turned in their work on time, the teacher promised them a free reading period. But if one student failed to hand in her work on time, none of the students could have time for free reading.

Fortune-Teller

Description

This activity will give students the opportunity to make predictions based on descriptions of different characters and their particular situations. Each team of students will receive a description of a character and the character's current situation in the form of a "fortune request." Students will act as fortune-tellers and collaborate to write a fortune for that character.

Skills/State Standards
✗ Making predictions
✗ Analyzing character

Materials You Need

- *Fortune-Teller* reproducible (page 92)
- Overhead projector and supplies

Getting Ready

Copy the sample fortune request below onto a transparency. Use this to model the activity.

Sample Fortune Request

Name: Haley

Gender: F

Age: 21

Describe Yourself: impulsive, proud, go-getter

Current Problem or Situation: My boss insulted me and now I hate working for her. I need to have a job right now, though.

Next, make photocopies of the *Fortune-Teller* reproducible. You will need to prepare at least one fortune request for each team of three or four students. Using the examples below to get you started, complete and cut out the forms.

Fortune Request #1
Name: Jolene
Gender: F
Age: 14
Describe Yourself: determined, quiet, very confident
Current Problem or Situation: My swim coach hasn't decided whether to let me swim in a big meet. He wants to let a senior swim because she's going to graduate. I know I'm the better swimmer. I just need the chance to swim in big meets to prove it.

Fortune Request #2
Name: David
Gender: M
Age: 12
Describe Yourself: sincere, outgoing, close to my friends and family
Current Problem or Situation: A really good friend is having an all-day, outdoor birthday party in the country this weekend. If I ask my parents if I can go, I'm afraid they won't let me. I think I might lie to them about where I am, which I don't want to do. But I really want to go to my friend's party.

Introducing the Activity

Remind students that they make predictions about things that will happen every day. Explain that good reading comprehension also involves making predictions. Suggest that making predictions for characters in stories is sort of like telling their fortunes.

Explain that in this activity, each team of students will get a fortune request from a different character. Given certain key information about the characters, students will predict how their characters will handle various situations. Each team will write down a brief fortune predicting what their character will do.

Modeling the Activity

Show students the sample fortune request using an overhead projector. Discuss as a class what a person like Haley would probably do in the given situation. Ask students to explain their answers.

Activity in Practice

1. Divide the class into teams of three or four students. Give each team a different fortune request.

2. Allow teams a few minutes to read and discuss the requests. Then, tell students to begin writing brief fortunes for their characters.

3. When teams are done writing, regroup as a class. Ask a volunteer from each team to read aloud their character's fortune-request form and the fortune the team wrote, explaining why those predictions were made. Encourage the class to discuss the different characters and their fortunes.

Extension

This activity could also be based on characters and situations from stories students will read in class. After reading the story, have students compare actual events from the story to the fortunes they predicted.

Tell It Like It Is

Description

This activity will give students the opportunity to practice making brief summaries of a text. Students will work in pairs to create their one-minute summaries and then present them to the class. The class will vote to decide which summaries were the best.

Skills/State Standards

X Summarizing and paraphrasing

X Comparing and contrasting

Materials You Need

- Stopwatches or watches with second hands
- Notebook paper
- Texts for the modeling segment and activity itself

Getting Ready

Decide in advance if you are going to use this activity with an expository or fictional text. Then, select a sample text with which students are familiar to model this activity. Prepare a one-minute summary of the text to share with students.

Select another text to use for the activity itself. The first time you do this activity, you may want to choose a text that students have previously read. Later on, for more of a challenge, you could have them summarize a text that is unfamiliar. Either way, it may be helpful for students to have copies of the text as a reference when writing their summaries. You will need one copy for every two students.

Introducing the Activity

Tell students that being able to summarize something briefly is important for reading, writing, and conversation. Suggest a few ways in which students provide brief summaries every day, such as telling a friend about a movie or recounting a phone call. Ask students if they can think of other instances when summarizing is used.

Explain that in this activity, students will have one minute to provide a brief summary of the text in question. They will work with partners to draft and practice reading the summary. Then, one student from each pair will present the summary to the class. After all of the summaries have been read, students will discuss the similarities and differences among them, and then vote on which summary was the most accurate and engaging.

Modeling the Activity

Start the clock and read your one-minute example of a text that is familiar to students. When you are finished, ask students to consider why you included certain elements and omitted others. Are there any details you could have left out or others that you should have included? Discuss the features of a good summary.

Activity in Practice

1. Divide the class into teams of two students. Locate a stopwatch or watch with a second hand for each team to use.

2. If needed, give students copies of the text they will be summarizing, along with sheets of notebook paper for writing their summaries. Tell students how much time they will have to draft their summaries. Be sure to allow enough time for students to practice reading their summaries aloud. Emphasize that each summary should only last one minute.

3. Once their summaries are complete, students can begin making their presentations, allowing one minute for each. Encourage the other students to take notes as they listen, jotting down important points that each summary missed or information it included that others did not.

4. Finally, have a discussion about the summaries and take a vote on which account included the most important information in the minute that was allowed.

Extensions

This activity can be used with different kinds of texts of varying levels of difficulty. To give students more of a challenge, for example, have them summarize an information-packed expository passage rather than the plot of a story.

Alternatively, ask students to create summaries of movies (real or imagined). Then, students may vote on which movie they would most like to watch.

Tell Me About It

Description

This activity combines several skills into one game-show format, requiring students to take on the role of authors.

Each pair of students will be given a short expository text, such as a newspaper article or chapter from a textbook. Their job will be to look for and identify the author's purpose, facts and opinions, and the author's perspective, based on the opinions found.

Skills/State Standards

✗ Understanding the author's purpose

✗ Identifying the author's perspective

✗ Distinguishing fact from opinion

Students will then create lists of short excerpts or paraphrased statements to be read aloud to the class in a game-show format. The class will be divided into three groups: contestants, authors, and audience members. One student from each pair will play the "author" and read his statements to the contestants. As the game show host, you will ask a question related to each statement, such as "Is that a fact?" or "Why did the author write this?" or "What do you think the author thinks?" The contestants must listen carefully in order to decide the nature of each statement—whether it is a fact or an opinion, a sentence that shows the author's perspective, or a sentence that reveals the purpose of the text.

Materials You Need

- Short expository texts (one for modeling and a different text for each pair of students)
- Index cards
- Overhead projector and supplies

Getting Ready

Although the activity is written for pairs of students, you could also have students work individually to give them more practice using these skills on their own. If students work in pairs, make sure that they each write the same number of statements so that they can take turns playing the author.

You may need to play several rounds of the game in order to give each student a chance to be a contestant, an audience member, and an author. Keep this in mind as you plan a schedule for the activity.

Select several short expository texts to use for the activity. Choose one to use when modeling the activity and copy it onto a transparency. Provide paper copies of the other texts—you will need a different text for each pair of students.

Finally, prepare a series of statements taken from a short text that students have not read. The statements should demonstrate the author's purpose, the author's perspective, and facts or opinions. Copy these statements onto a transparency to use during the modeling segment.

Introducing the Activity

Ask students to consider why authors write. What is the point of writing about something? After discussing the students' ideas, review the four major purposes of writing: to inform, to influence, to express, and to entertain.

Remind students that the purpose of a text is often related to the author's perspective on a subject. For example, if students read a chapter from a social studies textbook, what would they guess is the author's purpose? What about the author's perspective on the information? How would that author's perspective be different, or at least more evident, if the text was in the form of a political cartoon or a letter to the editor?

Tell students that in this activity, they will study expository texts to help them "get into the minds" of the authors. Then, they will portray those authors in a game show format. Using statements from the texts, the "authors" will try to stump contestants about their texts. The statements and follow-up questions will deal with the author's purpose, the author's perspective, and fact versus opinion. The contestants' job will be to identify each statement correctly. Explain that each student will get a chance to be an author, a contestant, and an audience member during the course of the activity.

Modeling the Activity

1. Place your transparency of a short expository text on the overhead projector. Read the text together as a class.

2. As you go through the text with students, ask them to point out statements from the text that are facts or opinions, that deal with the author's perspective, and that demonstrate the text's purpose. Underline these statements on the transparency. Paraphrase or summarize the ideas or details as needed to generate a variety of statements.

3. Next, show students a series of statements from a short text they have not read. After reading each statement, ask students to identify whether it stated a fact or an opinion, explained the author's purpose, or revealed the author's perspective.

4. You may wish to follow up some of the statements with simple questions, if applicable. Use these questions as a guide:

   - Fact—"Is that a fact?"
   - Opinion—"What do you think the author thinks?"
   - Perspective—"What is the author's perspective on the issue?"
   - Purpose—"What is the purpose of this text?"

5. Explain to students that with their partners they will look through a text and pull out excerpts that reveal these four elements. Then, playing the role of author, they will use the excerpts as the basis for making statements to the contestants and audience. The contestants' job will be to identify the type of statement and answer correctly any follow-up questions posed by the game show host.

Activity in Practice

1. Divide the class into teams of two students. Distribute a different text to each team. As students read through their texts, have them pull out quotations and paraphrase sentences to use for the game show and write those statements on index cards.

2. Next, divide the class into three groups: authors, contestants, and audience members. Explain that you will play three or more rounds of the game so that every student will have a chance to play each role.

3. Before you begin, review the basic format of the game:

   - The host (teacher) calls on an author to read a statement for the contestants.
   - The host asks a follow-up question of the contestants, if applicable.
   - The contestants identify the type of statement and win points for each correct response.
   - The audience members watch the game, attempting to answer the questions silently as practice for when they are contestants.

4. Once students seem comfortable with the format of the game, begin play.

5. After all of the students have had a chance to rotate into each role, have a discussion about how playing the game helped them determine a text's purpose as well as the author's perspective. Discuss how looking for facts and opinions can also play a part in determining the author's purpose and attitudes.

Extension

This game can also be played by matching up two pairs of students. Have the pairs take turns reading aloud their statements and questions to each other. Then, have pairs rotate among others in the class until all pairs have played the game with every other pair.

Webmasters

Part 1. Use the rubric to help you list below all of the features your Web site should contain.

_____ _____ _____

_____ _____ _____

_____ _____ _____

_____ _____ _____

_____ _____ _____

Part 2. List the major elements of a story in the first column. Then, list the specifics related to your story in the second column. In the third column, list the elements you have decided to include on your Web site.

Major Story Elements and Features	Your Story's Elements and Features	Elements and Features to Include on Your Web Site

Part 3. Use the back of this sheet to sketch out what your Web site might look like, based on the information from Parts 1 and 2 above.

Literary Logos

Title of story/text: _____

Step 1. Determine the Main Idea

Write the main idea of the story or text in the T-shirt outline below.

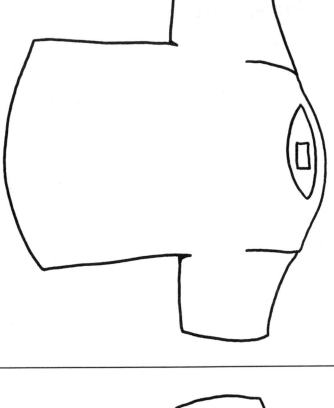

Step 2. Identify Supporting Details

Read through the story or text, looking for supporting details. Record the details in the T-shirt outline below.

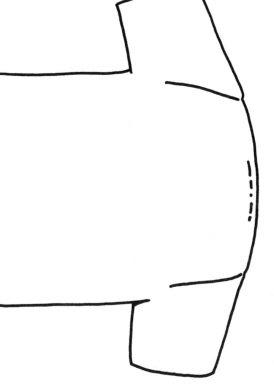

Step 3. Design Your Literary Logo

Share your ideas with other members of your team. Then, use a separate sheet of paper to come up with a T-shirt design based on the main idea and supporting details of the story or text.

Perfect Pitch

Title of story: _____

Part 1. Teaser Pitch

Work with your partner to draft a teaser pitch based on your story.

What to include in your teaser:
- **basis of story**   • **genre**   • **characters**   • **conflicts/twists**

First sentence:	
Second sentence:	
Third sentence:	

Part 2. Story Pitch

Use the space below to draft a story pitch with your partner. After revising your pitch, rewrite it on the back of this sheet or on a separate sheet of paper.

What to include in your story pitch:
- A logline or hook sentence
- Characters (heroes and villains)
- Conflicts (main plots, not too many subplots)
- Climax
- Conclusion
- Unique features
- Special details

_____

_____

_____

_____

_____

_____

_____

Laundry Line

Directions: Use the following patterns to create articles of clothing and accessories for the activity. Add other pieces as necessary.

Third Eye

Directions: Work with your team to figure out what each picture in the third eye might mean in relation to the story you will read. Write your predictions about the story in the corresponding space for each picture.

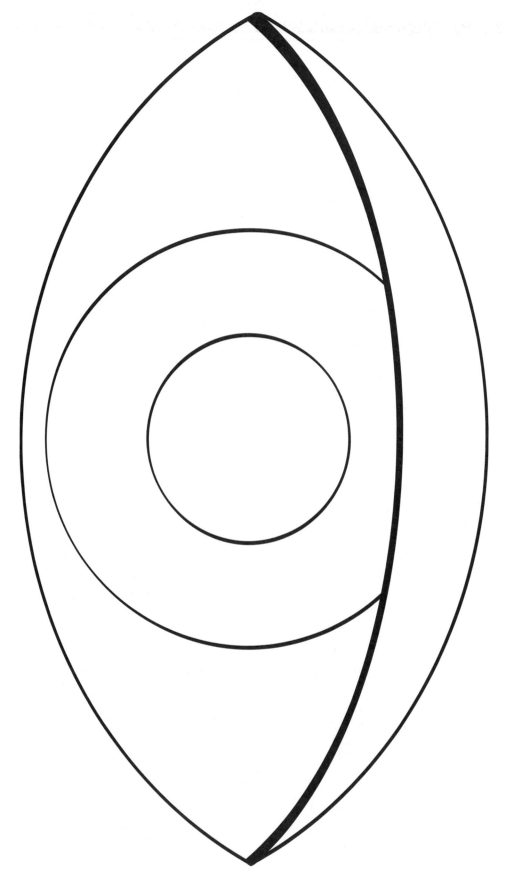

CD-2242 *Teamwork Test Prep*

The Great Debate

An **inference** is based on clues from the text in combination with the reader's own experiences. Inferences are not directly stated. A reader infers meaning based on what he reads in connection with what he already knows.

A **conclusion** is usually based on several pieces of information, including inferences. A reader can use inferences to help draw conclusions. Inferences tend to be specific, based on one particular clue. Conclusions can be based on a combination of inferences and other textual clues that relate to what the reader is trying to decide, or conclude.

A **generalization** is very broad, like a blanket statement, and can apply to any situation—not just the one that appears in the text. Generalizations can come from conclusions and inferences, or they can support a conclusion or inference, depending on the reader's reasoning process.

Got Your Back

Record the context clues given by your peers in the box. After reviewing all of the clues you have been given, decide on a meaning for your word and write it on the lines at the bottom of the page.

Word: _____

Context Clues

Definition: _____

_____

_____

_____

Fortune-Teller

Fortune Request #_____

Name: _____

Gender: _____

Age: _____

Describe Yourself: _____

Current Problem or Situation: _____

_____

_____

Fortune Request #_____

Name: _____

Gender: _____

Age: _____

Describe Yourself: _____

Current Problem or Situation: _____

_____

_____

Fortune Request #_____

Name: _____

Gender: _____

Age: _____

Describe Yourself: _____

Current Problem or Situation: _____

_____

_____

Name: _____

Date: _____   Class: _____

Directions: This test contains 5 reading selections and 36 questions. Read each selection. Then, answer the questions. Mark your answers on your answer sheet. Most questions are multiple choice. Be sure to fill in each bubble completely and erase any stray marks.

Sample   What is the BEST synonym for the word **valuable**?

    A   inexpensive

    B   noisy

    C   thrifty

    D   precious   **Sample**   Ⓐ Ⓑ Ⓒ ●

For some questions, you will be asked to write a short answer. Use the lines provided on your answer sheet to write each response.

Note to Teacher: This chapter contains a reproducible practice test based on the most common reading standards tested nationwide at the seventh-grade level. This practice test can be given to your students before, during, or after they have completed the activities in Chapter 5. (For a short diagnostic test, see Chapter 3.)

Practice Reading Test—Grade 7

Directions: Read the article. Then, answer questions 1 through 6 on your answer sheet.

Trees, Please

(1) Imagine this: You wake up, get dressed, eat breakfast, and then climb a tree. Sure, that sounds like a great thing to do—if you're a kid! But more and more adults are figuring out that climbing trees isn't just for kids anymore.

(2) Recreational tree climbing is a growing outdoor hobby, rivaling other popular activities such as rock climbing, cycling, or kayaking. And people of all ages are trying it!

(3) Peter Jenkins is one of many grown-ups who get a real kick out of tackling a tree for fun. Jenkins is the founder of Tree Climbers International (TCI), an organization for people who love climbing trees. Jenkins didn't start out climbing trees—he first tried rocks and mountains. However, his love for trees grew from his work as a tree surgeon.

(4) In 1983, Jenkins founded TCI to support others interested in exploring trees for sport and created a climbing school. This school offers training for people at all levels of expertise. Climbers take classes to learn the proper techniques for safe and effective climbing. The methods developed by Jenkins and his climbing school help protect both the trees and those who climb them.

(5) You might think that learning how to climb a tree is not necessary—it is something everyone already knows how to do, like tying your shoes or riding a bicycle. But climbing trees safely and effectively is important for the climber and for the tree's longevity. It starts with simple equipment: a helmet, harness or saddle, ropes, a throw bag and line, and gloves.

(6) Modern-day tree climbers use ropes to scale a trunk, instead of stepping on branches the old-fashioned way. Using ropes helps protect the trees rather than damaging them. The first step is looping a rope over a sturdy branch. If the branch is too high to just throw the rope over it, a throw bag is attached to the end of a throw line rope and thrown over the branch. When the throw bag is back on the ground, a climbing rope is tied to the throw line and pulled over the branch. Next comes the harness, or saddle, which the climber buckles on. To move himself higher into the tree, the climber ties a series of knots in a special sequence that joins the two ends of the rope together. The climber can pull himself up gradually, going high into the branches. This process is repeated until the climber reaches the branch over which the climbing rope is looped.

(7)   Even though adults have discovered tree climbing as a new pastime, kids still have an advantage. Since children and young adults are lower in body weight, they can pull their own weight more easily. Children as young as five years old have taken lessons in Jenkins' climbing school.

(8)   One of the greatest benefits to tree climbing is that it can be done at your own pace—literally. It is not a competitive sport and is something that can lift your spirits, as well as your body. So the next time you think there's nothing to do, try climbing a tree.

GO ON ➡

1 Read this sentence from the article.

But climbing trees safely and effectively is important for the climber and for the tree's longevity.

What does the word **longevity** mean?

A long duration of life

B height

C leafy branches

D flexibility

2 Tree Climbers International was started to—

F teach children to climb trees.

G support those interested in tree climbing.

H protect trees from deforestation.

J provide a way for tree surgeons to meet each other.

3 According to the article, recreational tree climbing is—

A a hobby only for adults.

B better than rock or mountain climbing.

C a growing activity among adults.

D a good way to take care of trees.

4 Basic climbing equipment includes ropes, gloves, a harness, and—

F a ladder.

G boots.

H a helmet.

J a partner.

5 Which of the following is a tree-climbing technique described in the article?

A using the branches as steps

B tying ropes into a ladder

C making a series of knots in the climbing rope

D having a partner pull on the rope

6 What is the main idea of the article?

F Tree climbing is a rediscovered hobby for all ages.

G Tree climbing courses are very popular among adults.

H Kids have an advantage when climbing trees due to low body weight.

J Tree climbing can be safe for trees if done properly.

Directions: Read the story. Then, answer questions 7 through 12 on your answer sheet.

Excerpt from
A Second Peep at Factory Life
by Josephine L. Baker

"Mill girls" was a name used to describe the young women, ranging in age from 15 to 30, who worked in the textile and cotton factories during the Industrial Revolution in the mid-1800s. These women were an important part of the textile workforce in Lowell, Massachusetts.

In "A Second Peep at Factory Life," a story written in 1845, mill girl Josephine L. Baker leads an imaginary visitor on a tour of the factory.

(1) There is the "counting-room," a long, low, brick building, and opposite is the "store-house," built of the same material, after the same model. Between them, swings the ponderous gate that shuts the mills in from the world without. But, stop; we must get "a pass," ere we go through, or "the watchman will be after us."

(2) Having obtained this, we will stop on the slight elevation by the gate, and view the mills. The one to the left rears high its huge sides of brick and mortar, and the belfry, towering far above the rest, stands out in bold relief against the rosy sky. The almost innumerable windows glitter, like gems, in the morning sunlight. It is six and a half stories high, and, like the fabled monster of old, who guarded the sacred waters of Mars, it seems to guard its less aspiring sister to the right; that is five and a half stories high, and to it is attached the repair-shop.

(3) If you please, we will pass to the larger factory—but be careful, or you will get lost in the mud, for this yard is not laid out in such beautiful order, as some of the factory yards are, nor can it be.

(4) We will just look into the first room. It is used for cleaning cloth. You see the scrubbing and scouring machines are in full operation, and gigging and fulling are going on in full perfection . . . .

GO ON ⟹

Practice Reading Test—Grade 7 (continued)

(5) In the second room the cloth is "finished," going through the various operations of burling, shearing, brushing, inking, fine-drawing, pressing, and packing for market. This is the pleasantest room on the corporation, and consequently they are never in want of help. The shearing, brushing, pressing and packing is done by males, while the burling, inking, marking and fine-drawing is performed by females.

(6) We will pass to the third room, called the "cassimere weaving-room," where all kinds of cloths are woven, from plain to the most exquisite fancy. There are between eighty and ninety looms, and part of the dressing is also done here.

(7) The fourth is the "broad weaving-room," and contains between thirty and forty looms; and broad sure enough they are. Just see how lazily the lathe drags backward and forward, and the shuttle—how spitefully it hops from one end of it to the other. But we must not stop longer, or perchance it will hop at us. You look weary; but, never mind! . . .

(8) Now, if you please, we will go up to the next room, where the spinning is done. Here we have spinning jacks or jennies that dance merrily along whizzing and singing, as they spin out their "long yarns," and it seems but pleasure to watch their movements; but it is hard work, and requires good health and much strength. Do not go too near, as we shall find that they do not understand the established rules of etiquette, and might unceremoniously knock us over.

(9) We must not stop here longer, for it is twelve o'clock, and we have the "carding-room" to visit before dinner. There are between twenty and thirty set of cards located closely together, and I beg of you to be careful as we go amongst them, or you will get caught in the machinery. You walk as though you were afraid of getting blue. Please excuse me, if I ask you not to be afraid. 'Tis a wholesome color, and soap and water will wash it off. The girls, you see, are partially guarded against it, by over-skirts and sleeves; but as it is not fashionable to wear masks, they cannot keep it from their faces.

(10) You appear surprised at the hurry and bustle now going on in the room, but your attention has been so engaged that you have forgotten the hour. Just look at the clock, and you will find that it wants but five minutes to "bell time." We will go to the door, and be ready to start when the others do; and now, while we are waiting, just cast your eyes to the stair-way, and you will see another flight of stairs, leading to another spinning-room; a picker is located somewhere in that region, but I cannot give you a description of it, as I have never had the courage to ascend more than five flight of stairs at a time. And—but the bell rings. . . .

[SOURCE: Josephine L. Baker, *Lowell Offering*, Vol. V (1845): 97-100.]

GO ON

7 In paragraph 1, the word **ponderous** means—

  A thoughtful.

  B heavy.

  C attractive.

  D solid.

8 According to the story, which of the following tasks is NOT performed in the second room?

  F brushing

  G packing

  H weaving

  J inking

9 In paragraph 2, the author compares the factory mill to a—

  A gem.

  B repair shop.

  C sister.

  D monster.

10 In paragraph 8, the author uses language to create a sense of—

  F playfulness.

  G confusion.

  H caution.

  J agitation.

11 Based on the author's description in paragraph 9, which of the following can the reader conclude?

  A The workers' faces are blue.

  B The carding room is where the workers relax.

  C The blue ink can leave permanent stains.

  D Long sleeves are required to work in the factory.

12 SHORT ANSWER: Please answer the following question on your answer sheet. Use complete sentences.

How do you think the mill girl feels about working in the factory? Support your answer with evidence from the story.

GO ON ➡

Practice Reading Test—Grade 7 (continued)

Directions: Read the article. Then, answer questions 13 through 21 on your answer sheet.

Big Stones, Big Mystery

(1) What do you think is the most remote inhabited place on earth? If you guessed a small island far out in an ocean somewhere, you are on the right track. Actually, it is *Te-Pito-te-Henua*, or as it is more commonly known, *Rapa Nui*, or Easter Island. The island lies about 1,200 miles from Polynesia, and more than 2,000 miles off the coast of South America. Because of its location in the Pacific Ocean, its climate is not tropical like other Polynesian islands—it is rainy and windy.

(2) But Easter Island is unusual for another, very baffling reason. Hundreds of giant stone statues, or *moai*, are scattered throughout the island—and no one knows who carved them or how they got there. These mysterious statues are figures of the upper halves of bodies, with exaggerated faces and long ears. They are carved from native volcanic rock that erupted from the ocean centuries ago; the rock is compressed ash, making it easy to carve. On average, the stone giants are 13 feet high and weigh 14 tons.

(3) These statues are not recent additions. The moai have been there, silently, for thousands of years, revealing very little. Since the first European explorers discovered them in 1722, these statues have been a source of awe and puzzlement. The remote location of the island continues to raise two major questions: what peoples made these statues, and what purpose did they serve?

GO ON

(4) Clues about the makers of these mysterious stones have been unearthed over time, with one of the most helpful recently discovered. Using both archaeological records and linguistic studies, experts speculate that the first inhabitants of Easter Island came from East Polynesia (not South America) between A.D. 400 and 800.

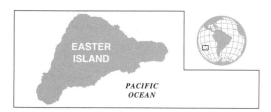

EASTER ISLAND

PACIFIC OCEAN

Although the first Easter Islanders, or *Rapanui* settlers, could have been from anywhere, since they had to reach the island by boat, it was language that helped pinpoint their ethnic origins. European explorers were very observant of the similarities among island peoples of the Pacific Ocean—most looked alike and could communicate despite the thousands of miles between their islands. The most salient clue came in the form of other bodies—skeletons discovered on the island in 1994. Through modern DNA analysis, the skeletons were identified as Polynesian.

(5) Researchers up to this point have partially solved the mystery by determining who made the statues—but the real question that still lingers is why. Lining the coast, nearly 300 moai stand with their backs to the sea, like ominous stone sentinels on watch. About 100 sit atop *ahu*, or sacred stone platforms. Although the design of the moai varies, the most uniform are located along the southeast coast.

(6) About 400 moai are still inside the island's quarry. This quarry is actually the inside of the Rano Raraku volcano. Overall, the island holds almost 900 moai, spread throughout the barren island. Since fewer than one third were ever placed on their platforms, more questions were raised about how these ancient peoples were able to move the moai into place. Some archaeologists speculate that transportation problems or lack of resources slowly put an end to a huge undertaking.

(7) Yet the purpose behind the statues themselves still lingers in the minds of visitors and experts alike. Based on Polynesian beliefs, archaeologists believe that these statues represent chiefs, ancestors, or other important males. Since the statues are very uniform in shape and size, some experts think that the moai are part of ancient religious practices. These statues could have been used in ceremonies to communicate with spirits, or could have been worshipped as part of regular religious practices. Since there is no written documentation and very little oral history, experts can only speculate based on what evidence they can find.

(8) Regardless of how they got there and why, the imposing stone figures of Rapa Nui are weighty historical relics worthy of further study and admiration.

GO ON ⟹

13 Easter Island is located—

A more than 2,000 miles off the coast of South America.

B next to the islands of Hawaii.

C close to several Polynesian islands.

D in the middle of the Mediterranean Sea.

14 Read this sentence from paragraph 5.

Lining the coast, nearly 300 moai stand with their backs to the sea, like ominous stone sentinels on watch.

What does the word **ominous** mean?

F threatening

G important

H curious

J huge

15 According to the article, the *moai* most likely represent—

A stone carvers.

B European explorers.

C tribal chiefs.

D volcanic spirits.

16 Paragraph 4 is mainly about—

F who discovered Easter Island in the 1700s.

G who originally inhabited the island.

H how archaeologists found new evidence.

J the common language shared by Pacific Islanders.

17 What information did experts learn by using the modern technique of DNA analysis?

A They discovered the ancient language spoken on the island.

B They determined the family lineage of tribal peoples.

C They identified island skeletons as being Polynesian in origin.

D They determined the specific use of the moai in the Polynesian culture.

GO ON

18 From information provided in the article, the reader can conclude that—

F the original settlers reached the island by swimming.

G a form of Polynesian language was spoken on the island.

H the statues were used to mark the island for incoming visitors.

J the island's inhabitants were successful in placing all of the statues.

19 Which sentence gives the BEST summary of the article?

A Easter Island would make an unusual vacation spot for the curious traveler.

B Although puzzling, Easter Island's mysterious past is slowly being uncovered.

C Ancestors of modern day Polynesians were most likely the first settlers of Easter Island.

D Easter Island is sprinkled with interesting stone statues representing ancestors.

20 The main mystery surrounding the statues is—

F the type of stone from which they were carved.

G the purpose they served.

H how the statue carvers reached the island.

J when the statues were made.

21 What is the BEST word to describe the author's attitude toward Easter Island?

A fear

B apathy

C wonder

D relief

Practice Reading Test—Grade 7 (continued)

Directions: Read the article. Then, answer questions 22 through 31 on your answer sheet.

All About Allergies

(1) Nausea, runny nose, itchy eyes, fever, hives—all of these diverse symptoms can be caused by allergies. Allergies can also cause swelling of the eyes, feet, or tongue. Extreme allergies can result in death in less than five minutes.

What Causes an Allergic Reaction

(2) Hundreds of thousands of Americans suffer from allergies. Common causes, or allergens, include pollen, mold, dust mites, pet dander, insect stings, and specific foods or drugs. An allergic person's immune system cannot tell the difference between the proteins in the allergen and the kind of proteins that could be carrying a deadly virus. The immune system responds to the perceived danger by releasing attack cells. The attack cells would normally attach to an invading virus and kill it. In an allergic reaction, they attach to normal cells, specifically mast cells and basophiles. These cells contain a chemical called histamine, which is released as the cells are destroyed.

(3) The release of histamine causes blood pressure to drop and the spaces between cells to fill with fluid. Depending on the location of the affected cells, this can cause stuffiness, nausea, hives, or any of the other allergic symptoms. The most severe allergic reaction, called anaphylactic shock, involves a combination of dangerously low blood pressure and severe swelling of the throat caused by extra fluid between cells.

How Allergies Are Diagnosed

(4) Most people who have allergies discover it on their own, when they find themselves stuffy or swollen or itchy. Sometimes, however, it may be unclear what is causing the allergy. In that case, doctors have two methods of solving the mystery. They often do a skin test. They put a small amount of a possible allergen on a needle and scratch the patient's skin. If the area swells to a certain point, doctors conclude the person is allergic to that substance. The other option is a blood test. Unfortunately, neither of these methods is 100% accurate.

Treatment for Allergies

(5) In the case of mild allergies, a medicine that blocks histamines can be enough. These medications, called antihistamines, allow allergic people to interact with pets and to function normally in the presence of allergens that cannot be avoided, like mold or pollen. People with severe allergies must avoid all contact with the allergen. Some people have such severe peanut allergies, for instance, that they cannot smell, touch, or eat even a trace amount of peanuts without having a reaction. Anaphylactic shock is treated with a shot of epinephrine, a steroid.

Practice Reading Test—Grade 7 (continued)

Allergies on the Rise

(6) Unfortunately, more and more people are developing allergies. Scientists are not sure why. One theory is that children are exposed to fewer natural allergens, such as those found in dirt, leaving them vulnerable to allergies later in life. Other scientists speculate that since we now import so many different kinds of food and plants from around the world, we are exposed to more potential allergens. Another factor contributing to the rising number of allergy sufferers may be that more Americans are opting for a vegetarian diet, which often includes peanuts. Some studies have even suggested that common plant allergens, like ragweed, grow faster and produce more pollen in the presence of increased carbon dioxide, caused by the burning of fossil fuels. It looks like, in the short term at least, we will be a sniffly, sneezy, itchy lot.

22 Which of the following BEST describes the passage?

  F   an article that explains how to avoid becoming allergic to something

  G   an article that explores various theories of the causes of allergies

  H   an article that focuses on new treatments for allergies

  J   an article that explores the causes and treatments of allergic reactions

23 What is the meaning of the term **allergen** introduced in paragraph 2?

  A   the immune system's attack cells

  B   the normal cells attacked by the immune system in an allergic reaction

  C   the substance that causes an allergic reaction

  D   the histamines released in an allergic reaction

GO ON

24 Which of the following is the BEST summary of an allergic reaction?

   F The immune system releases histamine to attack the allergen. The histamine causes blood pressure to drop and fluid to build up between cells.

   G The immune system releases attack cells which attach to normal cells. These cells release histamine as they die, causing blood pressure to drop and fluid to build up between cells.

   H The immune system attacks the healthy cells that usually keep blood pressure low.

   J The person has to take antihistamines to avoid getting sick. Low blood pressure and fluid between cells are side effects of the antihistamines.

25 Which of these common allergens is NOT mentioned in the passage?

   A mildew

   B pet dander

   C insect stings

   D pollen

26 Which of these symptoms is NOT commonly associated with a mild allergic reaction?

   F itchy eyes

   G very low blood pressure

   H nausea

   J fever

27 According to the passage, the most dangerous allergic reaction includes—

   A watery eyes and swollen throat.

   B low blood pressure and fever.

   C hives and fever.

   D low blood pressure and swollen throat.

28 Which of the following is NOT a theory mentioned in the passage to explain the rising number of people with allergies?

   F More people eat peanuts.

   G People take more medications.

   H People do not get exposed to natural allergens as children.

   J There is more pollen in the air.

GO ON

Practice Reading Test—Grade 7 (continued)

29 According to the passage, a person with mild allergies should do which of the following?

    A   avoid allergens and get a shot of epinephrine

    B   take an antihistamine and get a shot of epinephrine

    C   avoid allergens or take an antihistamine

    D   get an allergy test

30 Read the following four definitions of the word **lot**. Select the meaning that BEST matches how the word is used in paragraph 6.

    F   an object used in making a determination or choice at random

    G   something that befalls one because of or as if because of determination by lot

    H   a number of associated people or things

    J   a large extent, amount, or number

31 If you were to develop the passage further, what information would be most appropriate to include?

    A   the percentage of allergies that are life-threatening

    B   the risk factors of a vegetarian diet

    C   current treatment options and medicines being studied

    D   the medications doctors prescribe for hives

GO ON

Practice Reading Test—Grade 7 (continued)

Directions: Read the poem. Then, answer questions 32 through 36 on your answer sheet.

The Day Is Done
By Henry Wadsworth Longfellow

1   THE DAY is done, and the darkness
        Falls from the wings of Night,
    As a feather is wafted downward
        From an eagle in his flight.

5   I see the lights of the village
        Gleam through the rain and the mist,
    And a feeling of sadness comes o'er me
        That my soul cannot resist:

9   A feeling of sadness and longing,
        That is not akin to pain,
    And resembles sorrow only
        As the mist resembles the rain.

13 Come, read to me some poem,
        Some simple and heartfelt lay,
    That shall soothe this restless feeling,
        And banish the thoughts of day.

17 Not from the grand old masters,
        Not from the bards sublime,
    Whose distant footsteps echo
        Through the corridors of Time.

21 For, like strains of martial music,
        Their mighty thoughts suggest
    Life's endless toil and endeavor;
        And to-night I long for rest.

25 Read from some humbler poet,
        Whose songs gushed from his heart,
    As showers from the clouds of summer,
        Or tears from the eyelids start;

29 Who, through long days of labor,
        And nights devoid of ease,
    Still heard in his soul the music
        Of wonderful melodies.

33 Such songs have power to quiet
        The restless pulse of care,
    And come like the benediction
        That follows after prayer.

37 Then read from the treasured volume
        The poem of thy choice,
    And lend to the rhyme of the poet
        The beauty of thy voice.

41 And the night shall be filled with music,
        And the cares, that infest the day,
    Shall fold their tents, like the Arabs,
        And as silently steal away.

GO ON

32 What mood is portrayed in this poem?

    F anger

    G disappointment

    H happiness

    J melancholy

33 What literary element is used in the following lines of the poem?

Read from some humbler poet,
    Whose songs gushed from his heart,
As showers from the clouds of summer,
    Or tears from the eyelids start;

    A personification

    B simile

    C metaphor

    D symbolism

34 Complete the analogy as described in the poem: **mist** is to **rain** as **sadness** is to _____.

    F sorrow

    G longing

    H showers

    J pain

35 What is the meaning of the word **toil** as used in line 23?

    A sleep

    B worry

    C hard work

    D leisure

36 SHORT ANSWER: Please answer the following question on your answer sheet. Use complete sentences.

In the poem, the author makes comparisons between poetry and music. How do the reading of a poem and the remembering of a beautiful melody similarly affect the author? Support your answer with two examples from the story.

END OF PRACTICE TEST

Practice Reading Test—Grade 7
Answer Sheet

Directions: Record your answers on this answer sheet. Be sure to fill in each bubble completely and erase any stray marks. Use the lines provided to write each short-answer response.

1 Ⓐ Ⓑ Ⓒ Ⓓ

2 Ⓕ Ⓖ Ⓗ Ⓙ

3 Ⓐ Ⓑ Ⓒ Ⓓ

4 Ⓕ Ⓖ Ⓗ Ⓙ

5 Ⓐ Ⓑ Ⓒ Ⓓ

6 Ⓕ Ⓖ Ⓗ Ⓙ

7 Ⓐ Ⓑ Ⓒ Ⓓ

8 Ⓕ Ⓖ Ⓗ Ⓙ

9 Ⓐ Ⓑ Ⓒ Ⓓ

10 Ⓕ Ⓖ Ⓗ Ⓙ

11 Ⓐ Ⓑ Ⓒ Ⓓ

12 SHORT ANSWER: Use the space below to answer the question in complete sentences.

How do you think the mill girl feels about working in the factory? Support your answer with evidence from the story.

_____

_____

_____

_____

_____

_____

_____

_____

_____

_____

_____

13 Ⓐ Ⓑ Ⓒ Ⓓ

14 Ⓕ Ⓖ Ⓗ Ⓙ

15 Ⓐ Ⓑ Ⓒ Ⓓ

16 Ⓕ Ⓖ Ⓗ Ⓙ

17 Ⓐ Ⓑ Ⓒ Ⓓ

Practice Reading Test—Grade 7 (continued)

Answer Sheet

18 (F) (G) (H) (J)

19 (A) (B) (C) (D)

20 (F) (G) (H) (J)

21 (A) (B) (C) (D)

22 (F) (G) (H) (J)

23 (A) (B) (C) (D)

24 (F) (G) (H) (J)

25 (A) (B) (C) (D)

26 (F) (G) (H) (J)

27 (A) (B) (C) (D)

28 (F) (G) (H) (J)

29 (A) (B) (C) (D)

30 (F) (G) (H) (J)

31 (A) (B) (C) (D)

32 (F) (G) (H) (J)

33 (A) (B) (C) (D)

34 (F) (G) (H) (J)

36 SHORT ANSWER: Use the space below to answer the question in complete sentences.

In the poem, the author makes comparisons between poetry and music. How do the reading of a poem and the remembering of a beautiful melody similarly affect the author? Support your answer with two examples from the story.

_____

_____

_____

_____

_____

_____

_____

_____

_____

_____

_____

_____

Answer Key

Diagnostic Reading Test

1	C	9	A
2	G	10	J
3	B	11	A
4	H	12	H
5	A	13	C
6	H	14	F
7	C	15	C
8	F		

16 Lynn and her mother will most likely surprise Lynn's father with the guinea pig for his birthday present. Lynn and her father will care for the new pet together. Because Lynn's father raised guinea pigs as a child, he will likely share his experiences with Lynn.

Practice Reading Test

1	A	7	B
2	G	8	H
3	C	9	D
4	H	10	H
5	C	11	A
6	F		

12 *Answers will vary.*
The mill girl paints a bleak picture of the difficult life of a ninteenth-century factory worker. The factory gates are described as ponderous. They shut out the world and the factory is guarded by a watchman. The factory looks like monster, and its yard is barren and filled with mud. The mill girl realized the visitor is weary, but says "never mind"—she is probably used to working even though she's very tired. The shuttle hops spitefully; the spinning jacks and jennies might knock you down. She warns the visitor of getting caught in the machinery, of "getting blue" in the carding room, and to hurry up to start working promptly at "bell time."

13	A	25	A
14	F	26	G
15	C	27	D
16	G	28	G
17	C	29	C
18	H	30	H
19	B	31	C
20	G	32	J
21	C	33	B
22	J	34	F
23	C	35	C
24	G		

36 *Answers will vary.*
Simple poems soothe the author's restlessness. A humble poet's verse is compared to songs with wonderful melodies that have the power to quiet cares. Reading a simple poem seems to fill the night with music. In contrast, poetry from the "grand old masters" suggests life's hardships and warlike music.